Literary Byways of Boston & Cambridge

WITHDRAWN

Also in this series:

LITERARY
BYWAYS
O F
BOSTON
& CAMBRIDGE

Noëlle Blackmer Beatty

STARRHILL PRESS
Washington, D.C.

Starrhill Press, publisher
P.O. Box 21038
Washington, D.C. 20009-0538
(202) 387-9805

Illustrations by Jonel Sofian.
Maps by Deb Norman.
Hand-marbled paper by Iris Nevins, Sussex, N.J.

Library of Congress Cataloging in Publication Data

Beatty, Noëlle B.
    Literary byways of Boston & Cambridge / Noëlle Blackmer Beatty:
  [illustrations by Jonel Sofian : maps by Deb Norman].
       p.   cm.
  Includes bibliographical references and index.
  ISBN 0-913515-60-4 : $8.95
    1. American literature—Massachusetts—Boston—History and
  criticism. 2. American literature—Massachusetts—Cambridge-
  History and criticism. 3. Literary landmarks—Massachusetts-
  Cambridge—Guide-books. 4. Literary landmarks—Massachusetts-
  Boston—Guide-books. 5. Authors, American—Homes and haunts-
  Massachusetts. 6. Cambridge (Mass.)—Intellectual life. 7. Boston
  (Mass.)—Intellectual life. 8. Cambridge (Mass.) in literature.
  9. Boston (Mass.) in literature. 10. Walking—Massachusetts—Tours.
  I. Title. II. Title: Literary byways of Boston and Cambridge.
  PS255.B6B44   1991
  810.9'974461—dc20   9026071
                                                          CIP

Printed in the United States of America.
98765432

Contents

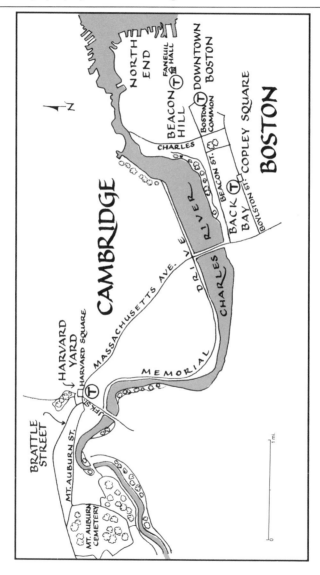

Introduction

WHEN Oliver Wendell Holmes placed the Boston State House at the "hub of the solar system," it came as no surprise to Bostonians—surely not to the Beacon Hill resident who was asked why she never ventured beyond Boston. "Why should I travel," she mused, "when I am already here?"

Actually, her apocryphal remark is not as outrageous as it may seem. All Americans—whether they realize it or not—have cultural roots in this tiny corner of New England, birthplace of the American Revolution and of American literature. Boston and Cambridge have nurtured literary talent for more than three hundred years, and it sometimes seems as if every writer in America has either lived or visited here.

This literary guide contains maps and tours of four neighborhoods in Boston and two in Cambridge, and thus serves as a practical guide for visitors. It will also appeal to readers who do not have time to stroll or are not lucky enough to visit, but still want to dip into New England's literary past.

The book opens with a walk around Beacon Hill, a unique corner of Boston that almost everyone wants to visit. If you are a stickler for chronology, however, you should start with the Downtown Boston and the Faneuil Hall-North End walks. Boston's earliest settlers lived there, before the watery outskirts of the town had been filled in. The far North End has always been high and dry, but ships once were able to sail almost to Faneuil Hall, off-loading cargo at neighboring Quincy Market.

Boston Athenaeum reading room

When the downtown area became too commercial, Boston's elite moved to breezy Beacon Hill, covering pastureland with solid brick homes. As the streets gradually extended down the western slope of the hill, they met marshy land at the edge of Charles Street.

After the land west of Charles Street had been drained and built on, developers conquered the swampy Back Bay, site of our last Boston walk. Here the sons and daughters of wealthy Beacon Hill families established a new order, building brownstone mansions in the latest style.

Across the Charles River in Cambridge are two more literary excursions. The streets around lively, stimulating Harvard Square have been home to writers since the early 1600s. Retreat into the quiet of Harvard Yard to recapture the past before you walk to the far reaches of Brattle Street. The elegant clapboard houses of Longfellow, Lowell and other Cambridge writers that line this tree-shaded street seem hardly touched by the twentieth century.

Notes for Walkers:

All walks begin at a subway stop, so be sure to take the "T" (short for Massachusetts Bay Transportation Authority). The subway lines are color-coded, and stops are marked on the maps in this guide.

The Freedom Trail is a well-planned walking tour of Boston's historic sites. The trail is marked by a line of red paint or bricks in the middle of the sidewalks. (On red brick sidewalks, the line changes to gray.) Free maps of the Freedom Trail are available from the National Park Service Visitor Center at 15 State Street and, in summer, outside Faneuil Hall—both of which are on the Faneuil Hall walk. Information about wheelchair access to historic sites is also available at the Visitor Center.

Finally, wear comfortable shoes. Cobblestones are a difficult surface to walk on, and the byways of both cities are full of them.

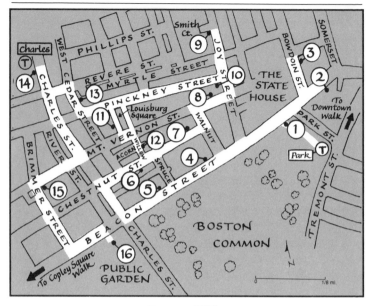

Beacon Hill

1. Shaw Memorial (Robert Lowell)
2. 10 ½ Beacon Street (Athenaeum)
3. 122 Bowdoin Street (John F. Kennedy)
4. 39 Beacon Street (H. W. Longfellow and Fanny Appleton)
5. 55 Beacon Street (William H. Prescott)
6. 50 Chestnut Street (Francis Parkman)
7. 13 Chestnut Street (Julia Ward Howe)
8. 55–59 Mt. Vernon Street (Nichols House Museum, Henry Adams, Thomas Bailey Aldrich)
9. 46 Joy Street (Museum of Afro-American History)
10. 4 Pinckney Street (Henry David Thoreau)
11. 10 Louisburg Square (Louisa May Alcott)
12. 9 Willow Street (Sylvia Plath)
13. 43 West Cedar Street (J. P. Marquand)
14. 148 Charles Street (site associated with James and Annie Fields, Sarah Orne Jewett, Willa Cather)
15. 44 Brimmer Street (Samuel Eliot Morison)
16. Mrs. Mallard and her ducklings

Beacon Hill

"T" Stop: Park Street (Red and Green Lines)
Restaurants: Charles Street

IN THE NINETEENTH century, Beacon Hill had it all: wealth, tradition, intellect and power. Those who didn't live here came as visitors because the drawing rooms of these red brick homes were places to see and to be seen by the writers, activists and historians who shaped American literature and culture.

The atmosphere and charm of Beacon Hill entice twentieth-century writers, too, though nowadays writers tend to live in converted stables, while their publishers occupy the grand mansions. Many houses on the Beacon Hill walk have historic plaques that describe noted residents and events. Walking time is two hours.

Enter the Boston Common beside the Park Street subway and take the path marked with a red line on the pavement. This is the section of Boston's Freedom Trail (see the Introduction) that leads to the SHAW MEMORIAL (1), across the street from the gold-domed STATE HOUSE.

Sculpted by American artist Augustus Saint-Gaudens, the imposing bronze bas-relief honors young Colonel Robert Gould Shaw and his regiment of black volunteer soldiers, many of whom died in a heroic attack on the Confederate stronghold at Fort Wagner, in Charleston, South Carolina. In 1990 the figures seen here came to life in the movie *Glory*.

Ralph Waldo Emerson, William Vaughn Moody, Paul Laurence Dunbar and John Berryman all wrote poems about "this boy soldier and his Negro band." Inscribed on the memorial are lines by the poet James Russell Lowell, for whom Shaw's "death for noble ends makes dying sweet."

Lowell's great-grandnephew **ROBERT LOWELL** (1917–1977) wrote his own interpretation of the monument for the 1960 Boston Arts Festival. In "For the Union Dead," Lowell refuses to accept his ancestor's glorification of Shaw's death, pointing out that the abolitionist ideals for which Shaw gave his life have not been fulfilled. A rich and complex poem, "For the Union Dead" transforms the Shaw Memorial into a symbol reflecting the futility of war and the failure of America to realize its promise.

Robert Lowell was born on Beacon Hill and spent three years as a child at 91 Revere Street. A gifted and driven poet who was a victim of a devastating series of mental breakdowns, Lowell produced a body of work that mirrors not only his own troubled life, but the illness of modern society as well.

A jog across Park Street leads to the **BOSTON ATHENAEUM** at 10½ Beacon Street **(2)**. Founded in 1807, the Athenaeum is a private library open to members, guests and researchers with prior permission. The upper galleries are ringed with books and furnished with antiques and orientals. Tours are given two afternoons a week by reservation, but not on Wednesdays, when the library tables are covered with white cloths and tea is served. The Athenaeum's wide-ranging collection includes some of George Washington's library and a number of volumes on Gypsy life and culture. An unlikely combination, perhaps, but the Athenaeum is an unusual institution.

The main branch of Goodspeed's Book Shop is at 7 Beacon Street. Selections from a large stock of rare books, prints and autographs are always on display.

JOHN F. KENNEDY (1917–1963) was Massachusetts personified, but he never owned a home in Boston. Instead, he rented an apartment on the third floor of 122 Bowdoin Street **(3)**. This allowed him to claim voting residence in the city when he first ran for Congress in 1946.

Profiles in Courage is Kennedy's account of courageous political actions taken by several members of Congress throughout American history. After the book won a Pulitzer Prize in 1957, a columnist accused Kennedy of taking credit for someone else's work. Theodore Sorensen, in his biography of Kennedy, recounts JFK's fury at the charge, which had been made on a prime-time television show. Together they collected manuscripts in Kennedy's handwriting and alerted potential witnesses for a confrontation. Both the network and the columnist soon recanted. Sorensen, who had been named as the supposed author, had his own revenge. It was he who drafted the network's "statement of retraction and regret."

Walk past the State House to 39 Beacon Street **(4)**. Here, in the drawing room on the second floor, Fanny Appleton married **HENRY WADSWORTH LONGFELLOW** in 1843. It was a great day for the poet-professor who had been wooing the beautiful young woman for seven long years. You will learn more about the Longfellows on the Brattle Street walk in Cambridge.

The old purple windowpanes of this house and its twin next door are prized by local residents. Some of these panes of glass have faded to a delicate, inimitable lilac. Others retain the strong purple hue that resulted from an error in the manufacture of the glass, when too much manganese was added to the formula. There are more purple panes at 63 and 64 Beacon Street.

WILLIAM H. PRESCOTT (1796–1859), who lived at 55 Beacon Street **(5)**, astounded his friends and earned an unassailable reputation as a historian with the publication in 1837 of his first work, *History of the Reign of Ferdinand and Isabella*. Although Prescott had previously published a few articles, he was regarded as a fun-loving literary dilettante. Moreover, he was nearly blind. A fellow Harvard undergraduate had hit him in the head with a crust of hard bread—a missile commonly thrown in dining-room brawls of the day—damaging his eyes so severely that he could read for only ten minutes at a time.

Prescott's buoyant personality was matched by a determined

intellect and dogged perseverance. He obtained unpublished documents from royal archives to prepare his accounts of the Spanish conquests of Mexico and Peru. To eliminate eyestrain, he took notes with a sharpened piece of ivory on the back of carbon paper; his secretary transcribed the copy hidden underneath. Eventually Prescott trained himself to dictate entire chapters from memory.

FRANCIS PARKMAN (1823–1893), one of America's most influential historians, lived at 50 Chestnut Street **(6)**. His victory over failing eyesight was even more dramatic than Prescott's. Parkman's eyes became so weak that he could read comfortably for only one minute at a time; "Prescott could see a little," he wrote a friend, "but I am no better off than an owl in the twilight."

As a student at Harvard, Parkman had yearned to write the "history of the American forest." So, as a young man with "Injuns on the brain," he slowly made his way west from Missouri along the Oregon Trail, only recently opened to settlers. *The Oregon Trail*, Parkman's account of this harrowing journey, started him on his life's work, a seven-volume history of the French-English conflict in North America. Parkman believed that the historian must be a "sharer and spectator of the action he describes." His vivid narratives based on actual documents set a new standard for American historians.

Famous actor Edwin Booth, brother of the infamous actor-assassin John Wilkes Booth, lived at 29A Chestnut Street. (Note the purple windowpanes.) Edwin was playing in a Boston theater on the night of Lincoln's assassination. He quickly canceled the show and slipped out of town.

JULIA WARD HOWE (1819–1910) moved to Boston in 1843, where her new husband directed the Perkins Institution for the Blind. In the early 1860s they moved to 13 Chestnut Street, one of a group of three houses designed by Charles Bulfinch **(7)**.

Howe's poem, "Battle Hymn of the Republic," was inspired by a visit to Union encampments around Washington in the early days of the Civil War. In *Reminiscences*, Howe recalls singing "snatches of the army songs so popular at that time" with her friends during the "tedious drive" back to the city. After singing the ballad "John Brown's Body," Howe told the others that she had often wished to "write some good words for that stirring tune."

She goes on to describe "the gray of the morning twilight" in which she "sprang out of bed" and "scrawled the verses almost without looking at the paper. I had learned to do this," she writes, "when, on previous occasions, attacks of versification had visited me in the night, and I feared to have recourse to a light lest I should wake the baby, who slept near me. . . . I like this better than most things that I have written," she thought as she fell back to sleep. The *Atlantic Monthly* liked it too and, on its publication in 1862, sent her a check for $4.00.

Howe's crusade on behalf of women's suffrage grew out of her work in the abolitionist cause. In *Reminiscences*, she makes her motivations clear. "The women of the North had greatly helped to open the door which admitted [slaves] to freedom and its safeguard, the ballot. Was this door to be shut in [the] face [of women]?"

HENRY ADAMS (1838–1918), a member of the intellectual and presidential Adams family, spent his boyhood at 57 Mt. Vernon Street **(8)**. (The **NICHOLS HOUSE MUSEUM** next door is worth a visit. This traditional Beacon Hill home, with its graceful spiral staircase, is open four afternoons a week.) On winter evenings, Henry studied Latin in an alcove of his father's study. There he listened to his father and friends plan ways to support the antislavery movement, for which they were "socially ostracized."

Adams left Boston in 1868 but returned two years later as professor of medieval history at Harvard, a post he initially refused because he "knew nothing about history, . . . much less about teaching, [and] more than enough about Harvard College." His learned and lyrical book, *Mont Saint Michel and Chartres*, centers a discussion of the art, architecture and civilization of the Middle Ages around the construction of these two great churches.

In his autobiography, *The Education of Henry Adams*, he

focuses more on his theories of history than his personal life and deals only indirectly with his wife's death by suicide. *Democracy*, one of his two novels, deserves to be better known for its humorous and pointed satire on the connivings of Washington politicians.

THOMAS BAILEY ALDRICH (1836–1907) moved into 59 Mt. Vernon **(8)** in 1885. A lighthearted, contented man, Aldrich wrote fiction and poetry that reflect his character. Aldrich's father could not afford to send him to Harvard, so he went to work in his uncle's New York countinghouse. When he finally moved north to edit a weekly magazine, Aldrich quickly perceived that in Boston literary talent meant more than money or social rank. "The humblest man of letters has a position here which he doesn't have in New York," he marveled. "The people of Boston are full blooded *readers*, appreciative, trained, . . . so a knight of the quill here is supposed necessarily to be a gentleman."

In *The Story of a Bad Boy*, Aldrich created the first realistic (and not moralistic) novel about the daily life of a rambunctious American boy. Writers from Mark Twain to J. D. Salinger are in debt to his humorous and nostalgic tale.

Aldrich was admired for his ingenuity and wit. He once mischievously remarked that Horace Scudder, his successor as editor of the *Atlantic Monthly*, was a greater man than Moses. Moses, Aldrich pointed out, had dried up the Red Sea once, while Scudder dried up the *Atlantic* monthly!

If you are short of time, you can walk down Mt. Vernon Street to Louisburg Square. Otherwise, walk on Joy Street to the "back" or north side of Beacon Hill. In the nineteenth century, these streets were home to the African-American and Irish women and men who cared for the houses and families of the more privileged. Pick up the Black Heritage Trail brochure, which covers many sites on Beacon Hill, when you visit the MUSEUM OF AFRO-AMERICAN HISTORY at 46 Joy Street **(9)**.

When you return to Pinckney Street, stop at No. 4 **(10)**, where HENRY DAVID THOREAU (1817–1862) spent a few years before his family moved to Concord. Thoreau is best known for *Walden*, the journal of his two-year stay in the cabin he built on Walden Pond near Concord. His statement of purpose is both simple and revolutionary. "I went to the woods because I wished to live deliberately, to front only the essential facts of life, and see if I could not learn what it had to teach, and not, when I came to die, discover that I had not lived."

Thoreau's essay "Civil Disobedience" formed the cornerstone of the nonviolent protests of Mahatma Gandhi and Martin Luther King. Thoreau refused to pay a poll tax in order to protest government policy on slavery and the Mexican War. The town of Concord jailed him overnight for the offense. Emerson, when he visited him in jail, asked, "Henry, why are you in there?" "Why are *you* out there?" Thoreau responded.

Louisa May Alcott spent time with her family in rented rooms at 20 Pinckney, a stone's throw from her last home in elegant Louisburg Square. Hawthorne lived briefly at No. 54. Like other Beacon Hill homes, No. 62 has a concealed room for fugitive slaves.

LOUISBURG SQUARE (the *s* is pronounced) is the heart of Beacon Hill. Its central patch of fenced park surrounded by gaslights reminds visitors of old London. The cobblestones you are tripping over, brought up from the beach, show no signs of wearing out.

When **LOUISA MAY ALCOTT** (1832–1888) moved her family into 10 Louisburg Square **(11)** in 1885, she had finally triumphed over odds that at times seemed insurmountable. Louisa and her sisters grew up in poverty, largely because her father, transcendentalist philosopher Bronson Alcott, spent his time discussing "chaos, cosmos & the Oversoul," as Louisa once put it, rather than seeking gainful employment. Although Louisa revered her father, it is clear that his inability to provide for his family shaped both her personality and her vocation.

The Alcotts lived in twenty or more houses before they finally settled in Orchard House, in Concord. Emerson, who admired Alcott's intellect, raised the money for the down payment and convinced others to help support the family. Luckily for Alcott, his wife adored him, but he was not what could be called a practical man. "Don't send Mr. Alcott for milk," she remarked: "He'll come back two days later driving the cow."

Louisa May Alcott worked as a teacher, and even as a household servant, in order to send money home. In 1862 she volunteered to nurse Civil War soldiers in Washington. In six weeks she gathered enough material to write *Hospital Sketches*, a financial and critical success that greatly encouraged her. In this time, too, she fell ill and was treated with calomel, a mercury compound that poisoned her (as it did countless others). The treatment also caused a bewildering series of ailments that left her in pain for the rest of her life.

Little Women, built around her own childhood and that of her three sisters, and set in their Concord home, rescued the family from poverty. Alcott longed to write dramas, love stories and mysteries. She did write all of these, but they did not have the public appeal or financial success of her stories of growing up. Of all these books, *Little Women* is the best and is still avidly read by young people. There is a reason: Jo March, one of the four sisters, is Louisa herself—an imaginative, impulsive, candid young woman who also knows that "food, fire and shelter are not *all* that women need."

SYLVIA PLATH (1932–1963) lived in 1958 just off Louisburg Square in an apartment at 9 Willow Street **(12)** at the head of tiny, cobblestoned Acorn Street. She and her husband, British poet Ted Hughes, returned to England the following year. Plath had a secretarial job, wrote poems and stories, and attended Robert Lowell's seminar at Boston University with fellow poets Anne Sexton and George Starbuck. After class they would have a drink at the Ritz before walking to the Waldorf cafeteria for a meal they could afford.

Plath had been hospitalized during college for a nervous breakdown, which she described in her coming-of-age novel, *The Bell Jar*. Biographers agree that Plath was psychologically unstable, that her marriage was strained and that she committed suicide at the age of thirty. They do not agree about the sources of her rage and jealousy, partly because her husband, poet laureate of Britain, has refused to discuss their life together.

Plath's poems are angry, bitter and passionate. During her year in Boston she wrote a more lighthearted one about the traditional Christmas caroling on Beacon Hill, saluting in one verse both the off-key singers and the hill's "odd violet panes."

Acorn Street, Beacon Hill

J. P. MARQUAND (1893–1960) lived at 43 West Cedar Street **(13)** in the 1920s before he became a best-selling novelist. One of his finest New England novels, *The Late George Apley*, is set amid late-night suppers of creamed oysters, in drawing rooms where citizens speak out against filling in the swampy margins of the Charles River Basin and other modern abominations.

As the story unfolds, the reader gradually discovers that the narrator of this "novel in the form of a memoir" is a humorless biographer who doesn't understand his subject. Marquand's book is, in part, a parody of the privately published memoirs resting on the library shelves of countless self-righteous Beacon Hill Brahmins. It is also, on another level, a sympathetic account of Apley's search for meaning in a life that he admits "has amounted to almost nothing."

Continue on to Revere Street, and turn left toward Charles Street. Now a stream of restaurants, theaters and shops, Charles Street once formed the western boundary of Beacon Hill.

Physician, essayist and poet **OLIVER WENDELL HOLMES, Sr.** (1809–1894) lived for a time on lower Charles Street. The site of his home is now a mass of paved roads. When Holmes was in his fifties, he left medicine to devote his time to writing. It was Holmes who characterized some Bostonians as "of the Brahmin caste of New England. This is the harmless, inoffensive, untitled aristocracy," he went on to explain.

Holmes was a brilliant, urbane conversationalist in the days when conversation was considered an art to practice and admire. In *The Autocrat of the Breakfast Table*, he assumes the role of a boarding-house patriarch who seizes command over the morning meal, delivering candid, chatty essays on such comfortable subjects as the pleasures of rowing or the events of a Harvard class reunion.

It takes an act of the imagination to conjure up the stately four-story house that was once 148 Charles Street, now the site of a parking garage **(14)**. In 1854 publisher and bookstore owner **JAMES T. FIELDS** (1817–1881) brought his young bride Annie Adams to his Charles Street home. You will meet James Fields again on the Downtown Boston walk. Both before and long after her husband died in 1881, Annie Fields welcomed writers, performers and artists whenever they were able to come. The shy poet John Greenleaf Whittier, for instance, would drop by for a breakfast chat after his early-morning walk.

Charles Dickens was so taken with the Fields's hospitality during his 1867 American tour that he left his hotel to stay with them. Annie Fields's diary for Christmas Eve of that year reveals the contented, yet candid, hostess. "Dickens came to dine and talked all the time. . . . Went to hear 'The [Christmas] Carol.' How beautiful it was. The whole house roared and cheered." To learn why they cheered, read about Dickens in the Downtown Boston walk.

HARRIET BEECHER STOWE (1811–1896), who lived in Boston as a young girl, often visited Annie Fields during the time her husband Calvin Stowe taught at Andover Theological Seminary north of Boston. Her major work, the antislavery novel *Uncle Tom's Cabin*, was then on its way to becoming a bestseller in America and Europe.

Soon after Annie Fields was widowed, she invited her close friend, writer SARAH ORNE JEWETT (1849–1909), to spend winters at Charles Street. Jewett, one of an influential group of nineteenth-century American regional writers, wrote *The Country of the Pointed Firs*. In this and other works she successfully captures the lives and conversations of men and women living in the rural villages of her native Maine.

When the two women went to England in 1898, they visited Henry James, who spoke to them fondly of his visits to Charles Street in his "faraway youth, when . . . I was so aspiring." Over tea, James admitted how much he admired the "elegance and exactness" of Jewett's stories.

Jewett's friendship with Annie Fields, like that of Henry's sister Alice James with Katharine Loring, followed a local custom, known colloquially as a "Boston marriage." It was not unusual for two single, upper-class women to share a home, and those who did were as socially acceptable as married couples.

The year after she moved to Boston, Jewett wrote "Tom's

Husband," a story with an interesting perspective on conventional marriage. Tom and Mary Wilson are newlyweds who agree to switch traditional roles; Tom begins to run the house, and Mary the business. The author comments that Mary "was too independent and self-reliant for a wife; it would seem at first thought that she needed a wife herself more than she did a husband." All goes well until Tom notices that his immersion in homemaking resembles "almost exactly the experience of most women" and that his "situation in life" is growing daily "more degrading." The story ends when Tom asserts his authority by insisting that Mary leave the business and travel with him to Europe.

One winter day in 1908 **WILLA CATHER** (1873–1947) was taken to Charles Street to meet Annie Fields, who wore "widow's lavender . . . with a scarf of Venetian lace on her hair," and Sarah Orne Jewett, who "looked very like the youthful picture of herself in the [card] game of 'Authors' I had played as a child." They "sat at tea," Cather recalled, in the "long drawing-room" on the second floor, which "ran the depth of the house, its front windows, heavily curtained, on Charles Street, its back windows looking down on a deep garden, . . . the Charles River and, beyond, the Cambridge shore."

Cather, who was then thirty-five, was in Boston on assignment for *McClure's Magazine* to rewrite another woman's muckraking biography of Mary Baker Eddy, founder of the Christian Science Church. Already a proficient writer of short stories, Cather had long admired Jewett's ability to place believable characters in a regional setting.

"Sometimes entering a new door can make a great change in one's life," Cather later wrote about that day. In their few months of friendship before Jewett's death the following year, Cather learned much from her mentor's careful and constructive criticism of her work. From observing the older woman's friendship with Annie Fields, Cather may also have learned that she was not alone in wishing to form a similar bond with a woman.

While Annie Fields was entertaining on Charles Street, a

young man named SAMUEL ELIOT MORISON (1887–1976) was growing up nearby at 44 Brimmer Street **(15)**. As a young man, Morison
was greatly influenced by the work of his grandfather's friend, historian Francis Parkman, whose house we visited earlier on Chestnut
Street. Morison is known for his definitive history of World War II
naval operations and his book describing the voyages of Christopher
Columbus, which he recreated by sailing the routes himself.

One Boy's Boston, 1887–1901 is another kind of book—a
quiet, unaffected memoir that rings absolutely true. Morison's
grandmother grew up at 45 Beacon Street in the mid-1800s with
"no plumbing of any description in that great house; all the water
had to be brought in from a well in the yard." The children "were
marched to the Tremont House once a week for a tub bath." At
that time the Tremont bedrooms were equipped only with a basin
and pitcher for washing. The hotel had, however, introduced "water
closets" and washrooms in the basement for their guests and eligible
Beacon Hill families.

Beacon Hill was dotted with horse stables in this period just
before the "internal combustion engine turned our economy upside-
down." Morison, who died in 1976, remembers riding his horse to a
Harvard teaching job, "tying him to a tree in the Yard, and loading
the saddlebags with students' papers that had to be corrected."

Several park benches await the weary in the Boston Public
Garden across Beacon Street at the corner of Charles Street. Fans
of Robert McCloskey's *Make Way for Ducklings!* (see the Copley
Square walk) should take the path leading from this corner to see
the pint-sized replicas of Mrs. Mallard and her family **(16)**. They
walked over here from Charles Street, just as you did.

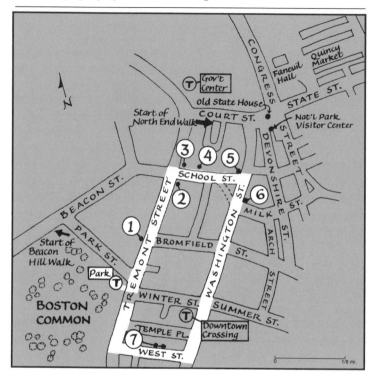

Downtown Boston

1. Old Granary Burying Ground
2. Parker House (Ralph Waldo Emerson, *Atlantic Monthly,*
   Charles Dickens)
3. King's Chapel
4. Old City Hall (Edwin O'Connor)
5. Globe Corner (Old Corner) Bookstore
6. Old South Meeting House
7. 9 & 15 West Street (Brattle Book Shop, Elizabeth Palmer Peabody,
   Margaret Fuller, Nathaniel Hawthorne)

Downtown Boston

"T" Stop: Park Street (Red and Green Lines)
Restaurants: On all streets

Hidden in downtown Boston are seventeenth-century burying grounds, the eighteenth-century launching site of the Boston Tea Party, and the gathering places of the nineteenth-century writers and intellects who made Boston the literary center of America. The Downtown Boston walk begins beside the Boston Common, land that was used as a pasture by settlers in 1622 and has remained open ever since. Walking time is one hour.

The OLD GRANARY BURYING GROUND (1) is next to the Park Street Church (look for the steeple). In the picturesque cemetery, placed in 1660 near the site of a grain storage building, are markers indicating the graves of Samuel Adams, Paul Revere and the owner of the most famous signature in America—John Hancock.

One Old Granary headstone is inscribed "Here lyes y body of Mary Goose, wife to Isaac Goose," leading some to wonder if they have found the burial place of the legendary Mother Goose. Others say that Isaac's second wife Elizabeth was the "real" Mother Goose. Iona and Peter Opie, authors of *The Oxford Dictionary of Nursery Rhymes*, put that idea to rest. The story, which they think was dreamed up around 1860 by a descendant of Mrs. Goose, is, they add, so "entertaining" that it "continues to have wide circulation."

Since their book establishes the early, European origin of almost all the rhymes, it is to Boston's credit that the four-stanza poem the Opies call the "best known four-line verses in the English language" was written by a one-time Boston resident, SARAH

JOSEPHA HALE (1788–1879). She wrote "Mary Had a Little Lamb" around 1830 about an incident that she called "partly true."

Mrs. Hale, an advocate of education for women, edited *Godey's Lady's Book* for forty years, retiring only when she approached ninety. First published in Boston, this instructive and influential magazine for women combined pages of fashion illustration and advice on household matters with works by Poe, Emerson, Holmes and Hawthorne.

The PARKER HOUSE, on the corner of Tremont and School streets, is the next landmark (2). Walk inside to view two cases of memorabilia installed in the lobby, including a broadside written by Charles Dickens describing "The Great International Walking-Match" and banquet he organized one February day in 1868.

RALPH WALDO EMERSON (1803–1882) used to board a coach on Saturday mornings in his home town of Concord for the three-hour ride into Boston. After visiting the Boston Athenaeum library, he dropped into the Old Corner Bookstore (now called the Globe Corner) on School Street, to catch up on literary gossip and invite friends for lunch at the Parker House.

He and his companions decided to gather one Saturday a month in a private dining room at Parker's, as the restaurant has always been known. With a logic that seems unassailable, they called their group the Saturday Club. Early members in addition to Emerson included almost all of that illustrious group of nineteenth-century New England writers with euphonious triple names: James Russell Lowell, Oliver Wendell Holmes, Henry Wadsworth Longfellow and poet John Greenleaf Whittier (a reticent Quaker who lived too far away to come often).

Members started meeting and eating their seven-course meals (including, of course, Parker House rolls) in the early afternoon. Conversation was even more important than food, and they kept at it as long as possible, though they had to stop early enough for Emerson and other suburbanites to arrive home before midnight.

In May 1857, a few members began to meet separately as the

Magazine Club, with the aim of starting a monthly magazine devoted to "literature, art, and politics." It was Holmes who suggested calling the new publication the *Atlantic Monthly*. They drafted James Russell Lowell as editor, and the first issue appeared six months later. Although the articles and reviews that appeared in the early issues were not signed, the names of the authors were an open secret in the tight literary society of Boston. Not surprisingly, many of them were among the magazine's founders. Now called the *Atlantic*, the magazine is still based in Boston.

In 1867 CHARLES DICKENS (1812–1870) stayed at the Parker House during his reading tour in America. A decade earlier, Dickens had conceived the idea of reading to audiences from his own works, noting that reading aloud "enables me, as it were, to write a book in company instead of in my own writing room, and to feel its effect coming freshly back upon me from the reader."

In truth, the excerpts were fresh, because Dickens recreated his own novels. He ruthlessly edited each chapter he intended to read, cutting some passages and rewriting others. He had the resulting "new" text printed in an inexpensive edition, which his fans bought and took with them to a performance.

Dickens prepared promptbooks from his own copy, underlining sentences he wished to emphasize. He also added stage directions ("moan," "slap the desk") at appropriate moments. Dickens didn't simply speak the words on the page, he acted every part with dramatic intensity. In fact, the readings were so demanding that they exhausted him, and so popular that thousands of fans lined up to buy tickets.

Across from the Parker House on the corner of School Street is KING'S CHAPEL (3). The 1630 burying ground on the far side of the chapel is the oldest in Boston; Nathaniel Hawthorne knew it well, and laid Hester Prynne and her scarlet letter to rest "in that burial-ground beside which King's Chapel has since been built."

The box pews in King's Chapel are superb examples of a Boston tradition. Each wealthy church-going family purchased a high-sided "box," which was warmed by a brazier on the floor and lined on three sides by benches. The ones here are comfortably upholstered. Those unable to afford these luxuries were seated "nearer to God" in the cold balcony.

Next to King's Chapel, set back from School Street, is **OLD CITY HALL,** now an office building **(4)**. This is also the original site of the Boston Public Latin School (hence School Street), the first public school in America. Samuel Adams and Benjamin Franklin began their education on this spot.

EDWIN O'CONNOR (1918–1968) sets his novel, *The Last Hurrah*, around a fictional City Hall, a "lunatic pile of a building" that strongly resembles this building at 45 School Street. Despite the author's disclaimer, it is generally agreed that the novel's locale is Boston and that its protagonist, Frank Skeffington, Jr., is modeled on James Michael Curley, Boston's golden-tongued mayor. Curley held so many state, local and national offices and had such a hold on his constituents that he is honored by an interesting double statue near Faneuil Hall. When he resigned in 1946 as U.S. Representative, his job was filled by another Irishman—a twenty- eight-year-old political novice named John F. Kennedy.

The Last Hurrah revolves around Skeffington's final campaign as mayor. A "cynical, outrageous, reprehensible" politician, Skeffington is also a mesmerizing speaker, a mentor to his nephew Adam Caulfield, and an "engaging rogue" who befriends the poor. O'Connor sees Skeffington's defeat as the coming of age of the New Deal. Franklin Delano Roosevelt's "social revolution," he makes clear, weakened the patronage power of Irish ward bosses and opened the way for a new kind of politics.

O'Connor, a radio announcer turned writer, wrote an even better Boston novel, *The Edge of Sadness*, about a former alcoholic. This story of an Irish-American priest determined to rebuild his shattered life won a Pulitzer Prize in 1962.

The **GLOBE CORNER BOOKSTORE (5)** at the corner of Washington and School streets is heir to the **OLD CORNER**

BOOKSTORE, which opened its doors in 1829 on this site. In 1831 a youngster of fourteen named Jamie Fields signed on as clerk at the Old Corner. He did well and made friends with William Ticknor, who soon took over the store. By 1854 Ticknor and Fields had become joint owners of the bookstore and of their own publishing company, installed in the same building. The company eventually became an affiliate of Boston's Houghton Mifflin Company. Ticknor and Fields started with Longfellow's poem "Evangeline" and went on to publish all the New England greats and Mark Twain as well. Writers, readers, lecturers, politicians, all gossiped and did business at the Old Corner with the blessing of its owners. If a writer didn't stop by, Fields took the initiative. He visited Hawthorne one day on a hunch. "How in Heaven's name did you know this thing

The Globe Corner (Old Corner) Bookstore

was there?" Hawthorne asked as he handed Fields an early version of *The Scarlet Letter*.

Their decision to offer royalties to British writers won them the loyalty of authors such as Tennyson and Thackeray, whose works had been pirated by American publishers for years. Fields also saw to it that Thackeray and Dickens visited Boston and enjoyed themselves in the process. There is no doubt that Boston owed its position as the center of literary publishing in nineteenth-century America to the imagination and zest of James Fields.

Bookstores should, of course, be admired from the inside, as well as the outside. Here you will find a wide selection of books about New England. Upstairs are enough travel books and maps to keep a determined explorer on the move for years.

Another bookseller-publisher named A. K. Loring had a shop at 319 Washington Street. Looking for a sure best seller, Loring advertised for an author of uplifting books for boys. One applicant was young **HORATIO ALGER, JR.** (1832–1899), a recent graduate of Harvard Divinity School.

Loring, who had already rejected the drafts of several hopefuls, fell immediately for Reverend Alger's upbeat, contemporary, Civil War story, *Frank's Campaign, or What Boys Can Do on the Farm for the Camp*. This adventure tale was one of a seemingly endless series by Horatio Alger about poor boys who boldly and honestly work their way up the ladder of success. The formula sold so many books that the careers of self-made men (and women) are still described as Horatio Alger stories.

In the spring of 1827, **EDGAR ALLAN POE** (1809–1849), then eighteen years old, met up with nineteen-year-old Calvin F. S. Thomas, whose Washington Street shop printed Poe's manuscript, *Tamerlane and Other Poems*. Thomas was not a publisher, but instead worked by the "job"—cash down for business flyers or works of literature alike. Poe, who had been born in Boston while his actor parents were performing there, was back in the city after a quarrel with his foster father about debts and drinking, both of which tormented him all his life. For reasons that are not known, Poe signed his work, "By a Bostonian."

Despite the fact that "Tamerlane" is an unexceptional poem, this slim book of verse has made history. Until 1988, only eleven copies were known to exist. That year a collector found one in New Hampshire, which he purchased for $15.00. Before the year was out, the book had been auctioned in New York City for $198,000.

Poe's fame hardly rests on this obscure book of youthful poems. He literally created both the mystery story and the detective novel. His settings are romantic, his characters are mysterious, and his plots are terrifying. For a long time, Poe was more appreciated by Europeans steeped in the romantic tradition than by his American contemporaries, and he was unable to make a living from his writing. He died in Baltimore, where he was found unconscious after one too many drinking bouts. There, on the anniversary of his death, an unknown, black-garbed figure for years made a midnight visit to his grave.

The **OLD SOUTH MEETING HOUSE (6)** at Milk Street is now a museum. Inside you can listen through earphones to a dramatization of the tumultuous meeting held there in December 1773 that erupted into the Boston Tea Party.

Continue on Washington Street past the busy pedestrian mall called the Downtown Crossing to West Street **(7)**. Inside the Brattle Book Shop at No. 9 are floors of old books, arranged by subject matter, and a helpful staff. Again, books related to New England are an important part of the stock.

The former home of **ELIZABETH PALMER PEABODY** (1804–1894) at No. 15 is now a restaurant. Elizabeth Peabody was an activist who, with her sister Mary, started the first kindergarten in America. In 1839 she turned the West Street front parlor into a bookstore, the first in America to offer books and magazines from France and Germany. Before long she had joined the growing group of Boston bookseller-publishers by printing works of Nathaniel Hawthorne and Henry David Thoreau.

In 1842 Elizabeth Peabody and Ralph Waldo Emerson
worked together at 15 West Street on *The Dial*, the quarterly journal
of the transcendentalists. Reacting against the dogmatic theology of
the day, Emerson, Thoreau, Bronson Alcott and others espoused
transcendentalism—a European-inspired but distinctly American
philosophy that each interpreted in his own way. Emerson, the
acknowledged leader, believed that independent and "self-reliant"
human beings should depend on their own divinely inspired intu-
ition to arrive at an understanding of the truth.

As a young woman, Elizabeth Peabody was unusual. In her
later years she was a legend. Henry James denied using the elderly
Miss Peabody as a model for Miss Birdseye in his novel *The
Bostonians*, but no one who knew her believed that his words
described anyone else. When James referred to "the unquenched
flame of [Miss Birdseye's] transcendentalism" and her devotion to
"the elevation of the species by the reading of Emerson,"
Bostonians saw only their own Elizabeth Peabody.

She made such an impression on the Boston literary world
that, in 1936, many years after her death, literary historian Van
Wyck Brooks allowed himself to imagine "Miss Peabody's future."
In his study of the period, *The Flowering of New England*, Brooks
"pictured her, forty years hence, drowsing in her chair on the lec-
ture-platform or plodding through the slush of a Boston winter, her
bonnet askew, her white hair falling loose, bearing still, amid the
snow and ice, the banner of education. If, perchance, you lifted her
out of a snowdrift, into which she had stumbled absentmindedly,
she would exclaim, between her gasps, 'I am so glad to see you! Can
you tell me which is the best Chinese grammar?' "

NATHANIEL HAWTHORNE (1804–1864), who worked at the
Boston Custom House, was a frequent visitor at the Peabody home.
Before he married Elizabeth's sister Sophia in the back parlor,
Hawthorne planned to invest his time and earnings in the Brook
Farm community, an experiment in group living that had been
planned at West Street. Members of the community sought to nour-

ish both mind and body by staffing a school and operating a farm in the countryside of West Roxbury (now part of Boston). Visitors such as Emerson helped to keep the intellectual atmosphere lively, but the farm eventually failed. Hawthorne left after a few months, writing Sophia that he had made a "gallant attack upon a heap of manure" but that married life there was not to be considered.

MARGARET FULLER (1810–1850) also lived on West Street during the 1840s. Intense and intellectual, she argued that women were entitled to the same rights as men, including that of higher education. Every Wednesday afternoon for five years, Margaret Fuller led "conversations" in Elizabeth Peabody's book-filled parlor. Twenty-five young women of Boston came to be instructed and to share in discussions concerning art, literature and music. Fuller's book, *Woman in the Nineteenth Century*, grew out of these meetings. Neglected at the time and forgotten later, this work touches on all the issues that eventually gave rise to the women's movement.

Margaret Fuller both astonished and surpassed her contemporaries. She left comfortable surroundings in Boston to become a reporter and literary critic for the New York *Tribune*. Later, on a trip to Rome, she met an Italian marquis whom she secretly married shortly before giving birth, at the age of thirty-eight, to their son. Three years later all three were drowned when they were shipwrecked off Fire Island, New York, on their journey home.

As you walk back up Tremont Street, put yourself back in 1890, when, believe it or not, carriages could hardly move through Boston's crowded downtown streets. This nineteenth-century gridlock was relieved by the nation's first subway system, which opened in 1897. A colorful plaque in the Park Street station tells the story of this National Historic Landmark.

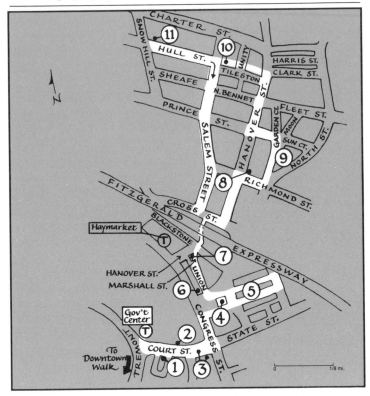

Faneuil Hall, Quincy Market and the North End

1. 26 Court Street (Nathaniel Hawthorne)
2. 17 Court Street (Benjamin Franklin)
3. Old State House and National Park Visitor Center
4. Faneuil Hall
5. Quincy Market
6. Union Street park (James Michael Curley)
7. Site of Benjamin Franklin's house
8. Site of New Brick Church (Ralph Waldo Emerson)
9. North Square (Paul Revere, Herman Melville)
10. Old North Church and Museum
11. Copp's Hill Burying Ground (James Fenimore Cooper)

Faneuil Hall, Quincy Market
and the North End

"T" Stop: Government Center (Blue and Green Lines)
Restaurants: Quincy Market area and the North End

THE FANEUIL Hall, Quincy Market and North End walk takes you through Boston's earliest settlements to the sites of the heady and dangerous days of the Revolution. Since many of the literary sites in this area have been torn down or paved over, you may want to stop for a snack and read about the writers who lived or visited here. Two restaurants have been around for more than a hundred years: Durgin Park in the North Market serves roast beef, chowder and baked beans at communal tables (cash only); the Union Oyster House on Union Street offers seafood at its curved mahogany bar. Daniel Webster ate there, as did Louis Philippe, exiled and impoverished heir to the throne of France, who, in 1797, gave French lessons in the low-beamed room upstairs.

This literary walk follows the **FREEDOM TRAIL,** described in the Introduction. Pick up a Freedom Trail map from the National Park Service Visitor Center across from the Old State House (No. 3 on map) or, in summer, outside Faneuil Hall. Walking time is two hours; one hour for the Faneuil Hall area alone.

As you exit the Government Center "T" stop, you can see the gold dome of Faneuil Hall to your right. Before going there, walk around to the back of the subway structure toward Court Street. One of Boston's treasures—the kettle of the old Oriental Tea Company—still steams cozily at the second-floor level of the building at the head of Court Street. An account of the day the exact capacity of the kettle was determined is posted in a window below.

NATHANIEL HAWTHORNE's *The Scarlet Letter* opens with a "throng" of Bostonians in front of the OLD PRISON, now 26 Court Street (1). They are awaiting the exit of the defiant Hester Prynne, who, with her infant daughter Pearl in her arms, is led to the nearby marketplace. There she is directed to "speak out the name" of the baby's father. "That, and thy repentance," thunders her accuser, "may avail to take the scarlet letter off thy breast." Hester's reply, "Never! . . . I will not speak!" sets the stage for Hawthorne's compelling study of innocence and guilt in Puritan New England.

BENJAMIN FRANKLIN was sent to work for his brother James as an apprentice printer at 17 Court Street (2). He grew up, you will see, not far from here.

After visiting the OLD STATE HOUSE (3) walk down Congress Street toward FANEUIL HALL (4) and QUINCY MARKET (5). Take a seat, if the weather is right, on the outdoor benches near Quincy Market (the one that looks like a Roman temple). The buildings on either side, South and North Markets, are filled with shops.

Faneuil Hall (people say Fan'l, though some argue that it used to be Fun'l) is Boston's beloved "cradle of liberty." Before you go inside, glance above the cupola at the copper and gold-leaf weathervane turning in the breeze. It is said that an American consul abroad once devised a fail-safe test for three stranded sailors claiming passage home to Boston. Only one passed, because he alone knew that a grasshopper sits atop Faneuil Hall.

Colonial craftsman Shem Drowne, who carved the grasshopper, lives on in Nathaniel Hawthorne's story "Drowne's Wooden Image." This fantasy about the mysterious sources of creativity takes place near Faneuil Hall amid "some of the cross-lanes that make this portion of the town so intricate." Hawthorne explored these streets while he was employed as weigher and gauger at the Boston Custom House. He was not happy in his "darksome dungeon," devoutly hoping that he could "find some way of escaping from this unblest Custom-House."

Before leaving the Faneuil Hall area, consider the story of

the African poet **PHILLIS WHEATLEY** (1753?–1784). In 1761 a young girl wrapped in a soiled piece of carpet was sold in Boston's slave market to John and Susannah Wheatley, residents of King Street (now State Street), not far from Faneuil Hall. By the time she was fourteen, Phillis Wheatley had learned both English and Latin and had started to write poetry. The Wheatleys gave her books, pen and paper, and a stove to ward off the winter chill. They even arranged for her poems to be published in England, where she was as admired for her accomplishments as she was in Boston. She eventually married a handsome grocer named John Peters, who "wore a smart wig and carried a cane," according to a contemporary account. This "proud and indolent" man ended up in jail for his debts. Phillis was buried with her newborn infant in 1784.

On your way to the next literary stop you will pass a small park running parallel to Union Street **(6)**, the location of the double statue of James Michael Curley mentioned in the Downtown Boston walk.

BENJAMIN FRANKLIN (1706-1790) lived as a child near the corner of Union and Marshall streets **(7)**. His father Josiah, a "tallow-chandler and sope boiler," allowed Benjamin only two years of formal schooling before requiring the ten-year-old to help in the family business. (Boston Latin School calls him its most famous dropout.) Benjamin's antipathy toward candle making and his avidity for books finally led his distraught father to send him to work for his brother James as an apprentice printer.

During the next five years Benjamin decided to improve

Faneuil Hall weathervane

himself. He read the latest English journals and worked to perfect his writing style. He tried writing poetry, which he later admitted was "wretched stuff." More successful were the articles he submitted anonymously to his brother's newspaper. The sight of his work in print, even if unacknowledged, partly made up for the beatings James rained on him for being "too saucy and provoking."

When James was jailed briefly for publishing an article that annoyed the colonial authorities, Benjamin decided to leave town. Franklin's candid and readable autobiography vividly recounts his two nearly disastrous sea voyages, his arrival penniless, hungry and dirty at a Philadelphia wharf, his beginnings as an independent printer, and the "rise and progress" of his political career and "philosophical reputation."

Walk on to the **NORTH END** (a lively Italian community) by following the red line of the Freedom Trail under the elevated Fitzgerald Expressway and beyond. Near the corner of Hanover and Richmond streets stood the New Brick Church **(8)**, the only parish church of Reverend Ralph Waldo Emerson, who preached here during his late twenties. A church history states that Emerson "was dismissed at his own request" after he realized that he had lost his faith in the sacrament of Holy Communion.

Continue on the Freedom Trail until you arrive at North Square **(9)**, the site of **PAUL REVERE**'s house. Revere, who was a silversmith, engraver, printer, bell maker, dentist, and Revolutionary courier, was *not* a writer. He was, however, the inspiration for "Paul Revere's Ride," Henry Wadsworth Longfellow's partially accurate and rhythmically satisfying poetic account of "the eighteenth of April, in Seventy-five."

Massachusetts writer **ESTHER FORBES** (1891–1967) wrote two books set in the Revolutionary period that are as compelling as they are true to history. *Paul Revere and the World He Lived In* is an adult biography; *Johnny Tremain* is a young people's classic about an apprentice silversmith who manages to participate in all the skirmishes from the Boston Tea Party to the battle of Lexington.

The North End was on high, dry land, and was accessible to navigable water. No wonder, then, that people chose to settle and build their first churches here. Across North Square is the small church (now Roman Catholic) that once was home port to a "hallelujah Methodist," a former seaman named Father Edward Taylor. HERMAN MELVILLE (1819–1891) modeled Father Mapple in *Moby Dick* on this spectacular orator, who "offered a prayer so deeply devout that he seemed kneeling and praying at the bottom of the sea." Father Mapple's sermon on Jonah and the whale goes on for nine pages—undoubtedly an accurate reflection of one Sunday's offering in Boston's North Square.

Richard, Increase, Cotton and Samuel Mather—men of the ministerial Mather dynasty—all lived around North Square. COTTON MATHER (1663–1728), who has more than four hundred books to his credit, bemoaned in one outburst "the Present Deplorable State of New England." His father INCREASE MATHER (1639–1723), who preached to Bostonians for more than sixty years, manifested fears that are remarkably contemporary. "Alas! Sinful Boston," he lamented, "dost thou not see, that Poverty is coming on thee like an armed Man?"

Follow the Freedom Trail to see OLD NORTH CHURCH, actually named Christ Church (10). Revere's lanterns as described by Longfellow—"one if by land, and two if by sea"—were hung from the steeple. In the museum-gift shop you can see a copy of the rare "Vinegar Bible," so named because an eighteenth-century typographical error turned the parable of the vineyard into vinegar. In another book on display, prayers for the royal family are blocked out and replaced by prayers for the president and the country.

COPP'S HILL BURYING GROUND (11) farther on has several gravestones from the 1660s. This lovely, tree-shaded site overlooking the water serves as a refuge for the hero of *Lionel Lincoln*, a Revolutionary War novel by James Fenimore Cooper.

Follow Salem Street (see the map) for a quick return to Government Center.

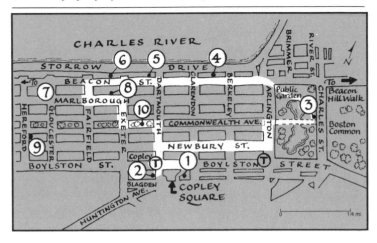

Copley Square and the Back Bay

1. Trinity Church
2. Boston Public Library (Mary Antin, Thomas Prince, Hamlin Garland)
3. Edward Everett Hale statue
4. 150 Beacon Street (Isabella Stewart Gardner)
5. 242 Beacon Street (Godfrey Lowell Cabot)
6. 302 Beacon Street (William Dean Howells)
7. To 91 Bay State Road (Eugene O'Neill)
8. 239 Marlborough Street (Elizabeth Hardwick and Robert Lowell)
9. 40 Hereford Street (Fannie Farmer)
10. William Lloyd Garrison statue

Copley Square and the Back Bay

"T" Stop: Copley Square (Green Line)
Restaurants: Copley Square, Newbury Street

SPACIOUS Copley Square was once a duck-hunting marsh. In fact, all of the Back Bay section of Boston was, in 1850, a watery mélange of swamp, mud and river. This walk visits historic Copley Square, smart Newbury Street, and Boston's three grand residential streets, where sober and substantial brownstones were built one by one as the land was filled in. By the turn of the century, Beacon Hill was passé; a new home in the Back Bay was *the* place to live. Walking time is two hours.

On one side of Copley Square sits **TRINITY CHURCH (1)**, built in 1877, not long after the swampy land was filled in. The interior of the church, a magnificent Romanesque building designed by H. H. Richardson, is decorated in red, green and gold and highlighted by stained glass windows designed by John LaFarge. Outside, the new and the old are dramatically juxtaposed. The reflection of the church tower ripples and soars in the glass wall of the adjacent Hancock Tower.

Solidly holding down the opposite side of the square is the **BOSTON PUBLIC LIBRARY (2)**. At its founding in 1854, it was the first free public library in the world to be supported by city taxes. The present building was completed in 1895.

"A low, wide-spreading building with a dignified granite front it was, flanked on all sides by noble old churches, museums, and school-houses, harmoniously disposed around a spacious triangle, called Copley Square." So wrote a young woman, to whom the library was "a palace." **MARY ANTIN** (1881–1949) emigrated from a village in czarist Russia to Boston in 1894. Poor and uneducated, but bright and determined, she grabbed the American experience as if it were the brass ring at a carnival carousel. She was so eager to share her transformation from ignorant peasant girl to educated city-dweller that she wrote her autobiography, *The Promised Land,* at the young age of thirty-one.

No amount of hardship could take Mary Antin's eye off the prize—education. The inscription on the Boston Public Library was, she felt, carved for her. "*Public Library—Built by the People— Free to All.* Did I not say it was my palace? Mine, because I was a citizen; mine, though I was born an alien; mine, though I lived on Dover Street. My palace—*mine!*"

Volumes from the library of **REVEREND THOMAS PRINCE** (1687–1758) are in the rare book room. The British found his col- lection in the steeple of Old South Meeting House when they turned the church into a riding school during the winter of 1775. The irreverent British stole Prince's copy of *History of Plimoth Plantation,* written by the Plymouth colony's first governor William Bradford. It turned up one hundred years later in London and now rests in the Massachusetts state archives.

Bostonian George Ticknor helped to build the first lending collection by donating his own extensive library. He then took lists of appropriate titles with him to Europe, bought everything he could find and shipped crates of knowledge home to Boston.

At the age of twenty-four, **HAMLIN GARLAND** (1860–1940) sold his North Dakota land claim for $200 and headed for Boston to "prepare myself for teaching American literature." He undertook his own education at the library and, like Howells, Cather, Stowe and Jewett, set out to write stories with distinctly American set- tings. Garland wrote about Boston in *Jason Edwards,* and in his autobiographical novel *A Son of the Middle Border.*

A window-shopping tour along Newbury Street leads to the Arlington Street gate to the **BOSTON PUBLIC GARDEN,** a good spot to relax and read about the rest of the Back Bay walk.

Make Way for Ducklings! by **ROBERT MCCLOSKEY** (b. 1914) has brought the Public Garden Lagoon into the lives of thousands of young people. Mr. and Mrs. Mallard's search for a suitable home for their soon-to-be-hatched ducklings and the new family's triumphant march from the Charles River to the Public Garden is the perfect adventure. Their faithful friend Michael sees to it that mother and ducklings are safely escorted across Beacon Street by four policemen "that Clancey had sent from headquarters." If you miss them (the Lagoon is filled only during the warm months), you can enjoy their likenesses in bronze near the gate they used at the corner of Charles Street (see the Beacon Hill map).

E. B. WHITE (1899–1985) set part of his book-for-all-ages, *The Trumpet of the Swan*, in the Public Garden and the Ritz-Carlton Hotel across the street. In the chapter entitled "A Night at the Ritz," White pays gentle tribute to the hotel's reputation for formal courtesy. The swan, whose name is Louis, plans to spend one night in luxury before his week-long engagement as trumpeter for the "Swan Boat man in the Boston Public Garden." When he tries to check in, Louis discovers that the reservation clerk's experience with performing artists has left him skeptical: "Actors are bad enough;" he groans, "musicians are worse." Louis, who is finally allowed to sign in as a "celebrity," soon proves his grasp of proper

Mrs. Mallard and her ducklings

Bostonian manners. Before settling in to spend the night in the bathtub, he calmly orders twelve watercress sandwiches (one with mayonnaise) from a bowing room service waiter.

Directly across the Public Garden (3) is a statue of **EDWARD EVERETT HALE** (1822–1909), a consistent champion of Boston's worthy causes and author of one of America's most stirring patriotic stories, "The Man Without a Country." It was typical of this "Grand Old Man of Boston" that he befriended the young Russian immigrant Mary Antin (whom we met in front of the Boston Public Library), setting her loose in his library to read and borrow any book she wished.

On the prestigious "water side" of Beacon, at No. 150 (4), is the home of Isabella Stewart (Mrs. Jack) Gardner, Boston's flamboyant patron of the arts. Her priceless art collection is housed at the Isabella Stewart Gardner Museum, where you can also see her portrait, painted by John Singer Sargent.

A literary comment from novelist **EDITH WHARTON** (1862–1937) may help explain why Sargent's 1888 portrait of "Mrs. Jack" in a low-cut dress was considered so scandalous that it was not publicly displayed until after her death in 1924. In Wharton's novel, *The Age of Innocence,* two New York socialites discuss the appropriate season to bring out their Paris dresses. "In Boston," one comments, "the rule was to put away one's Paris dresses for two years. Old Mrs. Baxter Pennilow . . . used to import twelve a year. . . . It was a standing order, and as she was ill for two years before she died they found forty-eight Worth dresses that had never been taken out of tissue paper; and when the girls left off their mourning they were able to wear the first lot at the symphony concerts without looking in advance of the fashion." "Ah well," her companion remarks, "Boston is more conservative than New York." Not so Mrs. Jack, whose Worth dresses kept Boston society buzzing.

The grand house at 242 Beacon Street (5) was owned by Boston Brahmin Godfrey Lowell Cabot, a prime mover in the **NEW ENGLAND WATCH AND WARD SOCIETY.** Working under an arcane state obscenity law, the organization was permitted to censor or ban publications or activities "manifestly tending to corrupt the morals of youth."

The society was founded in 1878 in plenty of time to warn Boston's District Attorney of the "obscene" content of a new edition of *Leaves of Grass* by **WALT WHITMAN** (1819–1892). Cabot perhaps did not realize, or care, that a Boston firm had already published some of Whitman's poems. In March 1860, before that earlier edition went to press, Ralph Waldo Emerson had invited Whitman for a long walk on the Common, during which he tried to persuade Whitman to eliminate some of the more graphically suggestive passages. Whitman refused, recalling later, "If I had cut sex out, I might just as well have cut everything out."

A 1925 article in H. L. Mencken's *American Mercury* magazine denounced the Watch and Ward Society for threatening booksellers. The author revealed that store owners were agreeing in advance to accept the society's ban rather than face adverse publicity. The public was intrigued, however, and before long the words "banned in Boston" guaranteed the commercial success of writers such as Theodore Dreiser, Ernest Hemingway, Sinclair Lewis and John Dos Passos. Upton Sinclair took up the challenge. His 1928 novel on the notorious trial of anarchists Sacco and Vanzetti was entitled *Boston.* It, too, was banned.

In his short story "A New England Winter," Henry James describes his heroine as "taking the inevitable course of good Bostonians" when she transfers "her household goods from the 'hill' [i.e. Beacon Hill] to the 'new land,'" in this case the "sunny side" of Commonwealth Avenue in the heart of the Back Bay. The opening up of this area is described so often in Boston-based literature of the period that it sometimes seems as if more characters in novels live in this part of Boston than novelists themselves. Coming up is the home of a man who built a new house in the Back Bay and then gave it to the hero of his current novel.

WILLIAM DEAN HOWELLS (1837–1920), who lived at 302 Beacon **(6)**, was a self-made literary man. He left a successful career in journalism to edit the *Atlantic Monthly*, where he had an immense influence on the American literary scene. He was a prolific writer of fiction, plays, poetry and literary criticism, much of which is neglected by modern readers. His reputation is secure, however. Spurning romantic heroes and larger-than-life Dickensian characters, Howells introduced realism, "the truthful treatment of material," to the American novel.

In *The Rise of Silas Lapham*, Howells describes the considerable ups and downs of a man with humble beginnings who becomes a millionaire Boston paint manufacturer. Lapham, who "always did like the water side of Beacon," decides to build a house for his family in the Back Bay. Howells began writing the novel while he was living in Louisburg Square on Beacon Hill and finished it after moving into his own newly built home at 302 Beacon. As he remarked to his good friend Henry James, "I shall be able to use all my experience, down to the quick." Howells and Lapham share a common hazard of building in the Back Bay: the fetid water pumped out of the salt marsh caused the neighborhood to smell "like the hold of a ship after a three years' voyage."

EUGENE O'NEILL (1888–1953) and his wife Carlotta lived for two years at 91 Bay State Road **(7)**. The O'Neills moved into Suite 401 of the Hotel Shelton in 1951. Too far away to reach easily on foot, the building is now part of the Boston University campus. Eugene, who was suffering from a degenerative disease, composed his own gloomy obituary: "Born in a hotel room—and God damn it—died in a hotel room."

O'Neill wrote dozens of plays, which were both honored (three Pulitzers and one Nobel Prize) and scorned (by many newspaper and magazine critics) during his lifetime. *Strange Interlude* is a 1928 experiment in which the characters speak their inner thoughts aloud in between their conversations with others on stage. The play received the ultimate accolade: banned in Boston. Its producers promptly removed it to a theater in nearby Quincy, where it was a sellout. Nine acts long, the play required an intermission, during which theatergoers looked for a bite to eat. Some of them, so New England lore goes, wandered over to an ice cream and hot dog stand run by a man named Howard Johnson. This may be one of the few instances in literary history in which an artist has helped launch an entrepreneur.

ELIZABETH HARDWICK (b.1916) and her husband, poet Robert Lowell, lived at 239 Marlborough Street **(8)** in the mid-1950s. In "Boston: The Lost Ideal," an essay published in *Harper's* magazine in 1959, Hardwick evokes the "fussy, sentimental, farcically mannered, archaic" figure of Marquand's George Apley to personify the "decline" of Boston.

Although Hardwick may have been unduly harsh in her attack, she set readers thinking about what she termed Boston's "mysteriously enduring reputation," which, in her view, has been undeserved since the 1890s, when Bostonians ceased to dominate America's intellectual life. Robert Lowell, too, was "awfully sick of Boston," by the late 1950s. "The only unconventional people here," he wrote a friend, "are charming screwballs, who never finish a picture or publish a line."

Turn on Exeter Street to Commonwealth Avenue, where the tree-filled center mall makes a perfect place to walk and admire the statues. Rest on a park bench and read about the former domain of FANNIE MERRITT FARMER (1857–1915), three blocks up the avenue at 40 Hereford Street **(9)**. The building is now a condominium and no statue commemorates her achievements, but Fannie Farmer's name remains a proverbial household word. Her revision of the original *Boston Cooking School Cook Book* has been continuously updated since it was first published in 1896.

Lively, red-headed Fannie Farmer was stricken as a young woman by a disease—possibly polio—that prevented her from finishing high school and left her with a pronounced limp. Looking for an outlet for her energies, she enrolled in the Boston Cooking School at the age of thirty-one. Five years later she became principal.

Sometimes referred to as "the mother of level measurements," Farmer banished the "heaping" spoonful along with lumps of butter "the size of an egg" from the kitchen. She preached "scientific" cookery and introduced imaginative recipes into an era of boiled dinners and white sauces. She thought her manuscript was good enough to be published by Little, Brown and Company, and she carried it there to tell them so. Somewhat cautiously, Little, Brown agreed to publish it at her expense. By the time they sold the rights to another publisher, the book had gone through eleven editions.

Between Dartmouth and Exeter streets **(10)** stands a statue of **WILLIAM LLOYD GARRISON** (1805–1879), editor of the *Liberator* and one of Boston's most determined abolitionists. Garrison was a volatile cross between fiery activist and determined pacifist. In the first issue of the *Liberator* he published his manifesto, the final words of which are engraved on his memorial. "I am in earnest—I will not equivocate—I will not excuse—I will not retreat a single inch—and I will be heard." At the same time, his pacifism made him refuse to encourage the active rescue of slaves.

Garrison was a "gentle and unassuming" man whose looks belied his activist bent. After viewing this statue, James Russell Lowell composed a couplet about Garrison's calm gaze.

> There's Garrison, his features very
> Benign for an incendiary.

We cannot leave the Back Bay without noting a novel that depicts Boston as it never will be—the utopian romance by **EDWARD BELLAMY** (1850–1898) entitled *Looking Backward: 2000-1887*. The novel's hero, Julian West, falls asleep in Boston on May 30, 1887, and awakens in the Commonwealth Avenue home of Dr. and Mrs. Leete on September 10, 2000.

Bellamy used the year 2000 as a vantage point for "looking backward" on the mistakes of the past and as a platform for advocating a form of socialism that would bring economic equity to all Americans. In the new society in which Julian West finds himself, corruption is a thing of the past. He is startled to find that there are no jails and no lawyers. He is even more amazed to discover that there are no banks either, because money is no longer needed. Citizens exchange work for credit and can obtain anything they need at government storehouses.

This serious novel has a few light touches. Veterans of a Boston winter can well imagine West's delight in "a continuous waterproof covering" that could be "let down so as to inclose the sidewalk and turn it into a well lighted and perfectly dry corridor." The young man, used to "the streets of Boston of my day [which] had been impassable, except to persons protected by umbrellas, boots, and heavy clothing," is impressed. Bellamy also has some prophetic ideas, such as "acoustically prepared chambers, connected by wire with subscribers' houses," which enable Julian and his hosts to listen to a Sunday morning sermon.

Despite its thin plot, *Looking Backward* was immediately popular, selling more than one million copies. Bellamy's book appealed to those who were convinced of the inner goodness of man and greatly influenced participants in the post-Civil War reform movement.

Statue of William Lloyd Garrison, Commonwealth Avenue

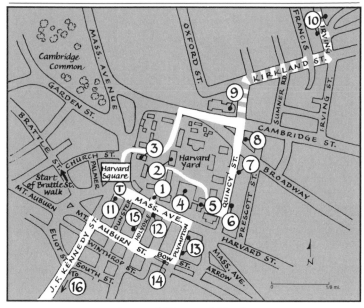

Around Harvard Yard

1. Harvard Yard gate at Holyoke Street
2. University Hall
3. Massachusetts Hall (George Pierce Baker, Thomas Wolfe, Eugene O'Neill)
4. Widener Library
5. Houghton Library
6. 16 & 20 Quincy Street (Richard Henry Dana, site of the James house)
7. Fogg Art Museum
8. Sackler Museum
9. Memorial Hall
10. 95 & 104A Irving Street (William James, E. E. Cummings)
11. Site of Anne Bradstreet's house
12. Site of John Bartlett's bookstore
13. 8 & 22 Plympton Street (Conrad Aiken, Malcolm Lowry, Richard Wilbur)
14. 44 Bow Street (Harvard *Lampoon* building)
15. Site of first American printing press
16. To Anderson Bridge (William Faulkner)

Around Harvard Yard

"T" Stop: Harvard Square (Red Line)—ten minutes from Park Street
Restaurants: Streets around Harvard Square

THE CITIES—and citizens—of Cambridge and Boston are so closely linked that a literary tour of one is not complete without a tour of the other. As you ride the "T" over the Charles River, gaze at the Boston skyline, look for sailboats and sculls, and listen for "Next stop, Haaavahd!" from the train's loudspeaker.

The Harvard Square subway kiosk is opposite the Harvard Coop (rhymes with hoop while you are in Cambridge). Next to the kiosk is an Information Center stocked with maps and bus schedules. The Out of Town News stand, housed in the architecturally interesting old subway kiosk, sells newspapers and magazines from all over the United States and at least fifty foreign cities.

All roads in Cambridge lead to and from Harvard Square— at least figuratively. (If you get lost in Cambridge, by the way, simply ask for "the Square.") The walks exploring literary Cambridge fan out in two directions from that central spot.

The Around Harvard Yard walk takes you through the center of Harvard College, and then back to the streets around the

Harvard Square kiosk

Square. The walk includes a bit of seventeenth- and eighteenth-century Cambridge, a selected group of Harvard writers, and sites associated with Henry James and Richard Henry Dana, Jr. Walking time is two hours; plan additional time for two superb art museums.

Enter Harvard Yard through the wrought-iron gate opposite Holyoke Street (1). Notice how quickly street noises fade as you walk into the tree-shaded, grassy Yard enclosure.

University Hall, with the statue of John Harvard outside, is the gray stone building straight ahead (2). The Reverend John Harvard's collection of four hundred books formed the core of Harvard's library until 1764, when the building burned down. The night before the fire, so the story goes, a student removed one book without permission. Realizing that he had the only surviving volume, the student presented it to the president of the college, who was grateful, but firm. He thanked the young man and promptly expelled him for his misdemeanor.

John Harvard's statue is a rallying point for demonstrations and serves as a marker for parading alumni at commencement events. The sculptor Daniel Chester French, who grew up in Cambridge, created the likeness. He had to imagine John Harvard's features, however, for no portrait of him has ever been found.

One of Harvard's legendary literary endeavors was the 47 Workshop, a playwriting seminar held in Massachusetts Hall (3) in the early 1920s. Professor George Pierce Baker's seminar attracted some of America's best young playwrights and fiction writers. Plays were produced in Agassiz Theatre, in the Radcliffe Yard, because Harvard had no theater of its own. This lack eventually led Baker to accept an offer to set up a drama department at Yale.

THOMAS WOLFE (1900–1938) took the seminar and later modeled a character in his autobiographical novel, *Of Time and the River*, on Baker, describing him as "a man whose professional career had been made difficult by two circumstances: all the professors thought he looked like an actor and all the actors thought he looked like a professor."

Wolfe's notebook for *Of Time and the River* is in the Houghton Library manuscript collection. It documents Wolfe's graduate-student days, when his loneliness and "ceaseless questing" led him to "enormous feats of reading" in Widener Library, which you will visit shortly. Wolfe, never a moderate man, describes his attack on Widener's shelves in the novel. Eugene Gant, Wolfe's fictional self, "would prowl the stacks of the library at night, pulling books out of a thousand shelves and reading in them like a madman. . . . At first, hovering over book stalls, or walking at night among the vast piled shelves of the library, he would read, watch in hand, muttering to himself in triumph or anger at the timing of each page: 'Fifty seconds to do that one. Damn you, we'll see! You will, will you?'—and he would tear through the next page in twenty seconds."

Baker's most famous student was **EUGENE O'NEILL** (1888–1953). In 1914, O'Neill persuaded his father—a notorious tightwad—to send him to study with Baker. O'Neill had already published some one-act plays, but he had doubts. In his letter of application, he wrote: "With my present training I might hope to become a mediocre journeyman playwright. It is just because I do not wish to be one, because I want to be an artist or nothing, that I am writing to you."

The portion of the Yard on the other side of University Hall is dominated by **WIDENER LIBRARY (4)**, which is as imposing inside as out. Harvard students mutter that its architect had an "edifice complex." Exhibits change often, but a Gutenberg Bible and a Shakespeare first folio of 1623 are always on view. A touching inscription accompanies the folio, which was produced by two actors in Shakespeare's company "without ambition either of selfe-profit, or fame: onely to keepe the memory of so worthy a Friend and Fellow alive, as was our Shakespeare."

Pusey Library (underground and to the right of Widener as you exit) holds the university's map and theater collections. **HOUGHTON LIBRARY (5)**, a small brick building located up a short

flight of steps, exhibits selections from Harvard's vast store of
manuscripts and rare books.

Quincy Street is beyond the gate at the far end of the Yard.
Cross the street, take a short jog to the left, and follow a paved path
flanked by two small posts **(6)** marked 16 and 20.

The yellow clapboard house at 16 Quincy Street was the
boyhood home of **RICHARD HENRY DANA, JR.** (1815–1882).
Severe eye trouble forced Dana to take a break from Harvard in his
junior year. The young man signed up as a crewman on a
California-bound ship trading in hides, a decision that foreshad-
owed his career as a maverick. His well-born friends were shocked:
they would never have signed on as a common sailor, and they
would have chosen a ship trading in furs—the only respectable
business on the high seas.

At the age of twenty-five, Dana published *Two Years before
the Mast,* in part the tale of his adventurous trip around Cape Horn,
and in part the story of his discovery of life itself. Dana went on to
become a lawyer and to write a definitive manual on maritime law
known as *The Seaman's Friend.* His heart remained at sea, with the
sailors he had befriended, and with all persecuted people. Dana
often donated his services as counsel for runaway slaves and for
Bostonians who had abetted a slave's flight to the north.

HENRY JAMES (1843–1916) lived for a time at 20 Quincy
Street, where the Harvard Faculty Club now stands. His family
home, Henry decided, was "about as lively as the inner sepulchre."
What he really wanted to do was to live and write abroad. Funds
were limited, however, and he was forced to wait until his older
brother William returned home from his own tour. In the mean-
time, Henry rode the horsecar into Boston, published stories and
criticism, and took long walks with his new friend William Dean
Howells. By the time he was twenty-six he was able to sail for
Europe to fulfill his dream.

Henry James is without doubt one of the greatest American
novelists. In an unusual twist, he is also one of America's best

known expatriates. He spent most of his adult life in Europe, and became a British citizen. As an old man, he confessed that he had a "superstitious terror" that Boston and Cambridge could "again stretch out strange inevitable tentacles to draw me back and destroy me." "I could come back to America . . . to die," he wrote, "but never, never to live." He died in England, but left instructions that his ashes be buried in the family plot in the Cambridge Cemetery beside the Charles River.

Wherever he lived and traveled, James was an observer par excellence. He wrote exhaustively and convincingly of the conflicts that arose when cultured, ingenuous Americans attempted to integrate themselves and their wealth into the ancient and dangerous world of aristocratic Europeans. *The Portrait of a Lady* and *The Golden Bowl* are early and late novels exploring this theme.

After his parents died, James shared a house for a short time with his sister Alice at 131 Mt. Vernon Street on Beacon Hill. Alice had by then formed a close relationship with a young woman named Katharine Loring. Their attachment is reflected in Henry's next novel *The Bostonians*, which James characterized as a "study of one of those friendships between women which are so common in New England."

In *The Bostonians* James casts a cold eye on the growth of the women's movement, in the context of a determined battle for control over a passive young woman called Verena Tarrant. The opponents are Verena's older mentor Olive Chancellor, a radical feminist reformer, and Basil Ransom, a handsome, not very intelligent young southerner. Basil wins in the end, but James is far from optimistic about Verena's future.

The story of **ALICE JAMES** (1849–1892) is a troubling one. "In our family group," Henry commented, "girls seem scarcely to have had a chance." Alice suffered her first nervous breakdown at Quincy Street when she was twenty. Her treatment was enforced rest and lack of stimulating activity—probably the worst possible prescription for an active, intelligent young woman.

Twenty years later in her journal, Alice described her descent into depression and suicidal despair in a poignant and yet slightly distant and ironic voice. "As I used to sit immovable reading in the library," she wrote, "it used to seem to me that the only difference between me and the insane was that I had not only the horrors and suffering of insanity but the duties of doctor, nurse, and straitjacket imposed upon me too."

Alice James was never offered marriage, nor encouraged to develop her curious mind or her literary skills. She lived the last part of her life abroad as a semi-invalid, cared for by her devoted friend Katharine. Her journal, which Henry praised for "its individuality, its independence," as well as its "beauty and eloquence" was not published for many years, in part because Henry refused to have the gossip he had amused her with made public during his lifetime.

Down Quincy Street to the right you will find the **FOGG (7)** and the **SACKLER** museums **(8)**, neither of which art enthusiasts should neglect, particularly as they are on the way to **MEMORIAL HALL (9)**. You can admire this imposing Ruskinian Gothic monument from across the street, even if you decide not to visit it.

Memorial Hall was built to honor the Harvard men who died for the Union cause in the Civil War. In *The Bostonians*, Verena tells Basil, a Confederate veteran, that Memorial Hall "is one place where perhaps it would be indelicate to take a Mississippian." Basil, however, is magnanimous, declaring it "the finest piece of architecture he had ever seen," even though "there was rather too much brick about it." Still, Basil thought, "it was buttressed, cloistered, turreted, dedicated, superscribed, as he had never seen anything; though it didn't look old, it looked significant; it covered a large area, and it sprang majestic into the winter air."

A few blocks beyond Memorial Hall, and probably too far for weary walkers, is Irving Street **(10)**, home to an eclectic mix of writers over the years.

WILLIAM JAMES (1842–1910), the eldest son of the James family, lived at 95 Irving Street. William was a medical doctor, as well as a psychologist, writer, philosopher, and beloved Harvard professor. One of his admirers was graduate student in philosophy **W. E. B. DU BOIS** (1868–1963), who wrote that James "was my friend and guide to clear thinking." Scrupulously honest, James warned the young black radical, "It is hard to earn a living with philosophy."

The poet **EDWARD ESTLIN CUMMINGS** (1894–1962) was born at 104-A Irving Street. A multitalented man, e.e. cummings, as he signed his work, was also a painter, novelist and playwright. The words and letters in many of his poems drift across the page in a way that imitates the pauses in human speech, or the lazy fall of a leaf. Cummings was clever, funny, sexy and sometimes superficial. He could be caustic about the stuffy and narrow-minded ladies of Cambridge, and he could also gaze in wide-eyed wonder at the mystery of life.

One of **JULIA CHILD**'s (b. 1912) well-equipped kitchens is at 103 Irving Street. Her books on French cooking, combined with her television demonstrations, have raised the consciousness of thousands of aspiring chefs and gourmets. Child's books and papers are deposited in the Schlesinger Library in the Radcliffe Yard.

The second part of this walk starts back in Harvard Square, which you can reach by returning through the quiet bustle of Harvard Yard.

America's first published poet, **ANNE BRADSTREET** (1612–1672), settled in a home at the corner of present-day John F. Kennedy Street and Massachusetts Avenue in 1631 **(11)**. Bradstreet did not let illness, eight children, or her later obligations as wife of a governor of the colony keep her from publishing more than four hundred pages of verse. The first book by this remarkable woman appeared in London in 1650.

Bradstreet's early verses deal with abstract subjects and are built on a formal, English tradition. Later, she began to write more interesting poems created out of her own experiences. One of these describes the night in July 1666 when she heard "that fearful sound of 'Fire!' and 'Fire!' " and gazed, horrified, as her home burned to the ground.

The University Book Store once stood on the corner of Massachusetts Avenue and Holyoke Street **(12)**. **JOHN BARTLETT** (1820–1905) started work there at sixteen. He was so good at his job that he ended up owning the store, which he turned into a gathering place for the local literati. Bartlett, who devoured every book he could lay his hands on, turned out to be a whiz at remembering what he had read and where he had read it. Whenever anyone wondered who said, "Lay on, Macduff," or where to locate, "Get thee behind me, Satan," a cry would go up, "Ask John Bartlett!" Soon Bartlett began writing down his sources from literature and the Bible "without any view of publication." His list proved to be so popular, however, that in 1855 he issued the first edition of his *Familiar Quotations,* which has been revised and enlarged periodically ever since.

John Bartlett also edited Izaak Walton's *The Compleat Angler,* and was so skilled a fisherman that James Russell Lowell was moved to dedicate a sentimental verse "To Mr. John Bartlett, Who Had Sent Me a Seven-Pound Trout." ("I see him trace the wayward brook / Amid the forest mysteries.")

Harvard Book Store at the corner of Plympton Street has a bit of everything. After you turn into Plympton Street **(13)**, you will pass the tiny Grolier Book Shop, which has specialized in poetry since 1927.

Books are a fast-selling commodity in this town. The Information Center near the subway has a list of Cambridge bookstores. You could also try Palmer Street, behind the Harvard Coop, which boasts both a travel and map store and the Coop book and record annex. Schoenhof's at 76A Mt. Auburn Street is a center for foreign books. Best of all, everywhere you go you will see stores specializing in inexpensive, out-of-print and recycled books.

Poet and novelist **CONRAD AIKEN** (1889–1973) lived for a while in an apartment at 8 Plympton Street. In a 1947 poem called "The Kid," Aiken memorialized William Blackstone, Boston's first settler, who lived on Beacon Hill.

The English-born novelist **MALCOLM LOWRY** (1909–1957) admired Aiken and, in 1929, settled in at Aiken's apartment to work on his first novel. He wrote his masterpiece, *Under the Volcano*, almost twenty years later. In this grim novel, Lowry evokes the fall of man as he chronicles the last day in the life of a self-destructive alcoholic (who, sadly, turned out to be Lowry himself).

RICHARD WILBUR (b.1921) lived at 22 Plympton in the late 1940s, where he completed his first collection of poems, *The Beautiful Changes*. Wilbur is a prize-winning poet who uses time-honored poetic conventions (rhyme is one of them) to create lyrical, and completely contemporary, verse. His translations of plays by Molière are accurate, witty and eminently playable on the modern stage.

The daily undergraduate newspaper, the *Crimson*, is located at 14 Plympton Street, not far from the offices of several other Harvard publications. Writers all over America consider their training on these publications as important to their careers as their college coursework.

The *Lampoon* humor magazine, at 44 Bow Street **(14)**, was saved in its early years by business manager and future newspaper tycoon William Randolph Hearst, who dramatically increased its diminutive circulation before his wild behavior got him expelled from the college. The *Lampoon* is housed in the "Castle," an amusing, anthropomorphic building reached by continuing on Plympton toward Mt. Auburn Street, where the brick structure sits on a pie-shaped piece of land in the middle of the street. Walk around to the other end to see the facelike facade, which cleverly suggests eyes, nose, mouth (the colorful door), and even a hat.

Harvard's literary publication, the *Advocate*, published the early works of such Harvard-educated writers as T. S. Eliot, E. E. Cummings, Wallace Stevens, James Agee, Edwin Arlington Robinson, Conrad Aiken, Adrienne Rich and John Updike. Norman Mailer's first story appeared in the *Advocate*. When the story won a magazine contest, Mailer gave up aeronautical engineering for the literary life.

Although novelist **JOHN UPDIKE** (b.1932) writes often about his home state of Pennsylvania and his years in Ipswich, Massachusetts, his roots are also firmly implanted in his undergraduate years at Harvard, where he lived in Lowell House, across from the *Lampoon* building. Updike readers who live in Cambridge and Boston usually feel completely at home in the unnamed cities of his novels.

In his story "The Christian Roommates," Updike describes a freshman's discovery of the "grateful pause" that arrives after mid-

Harvard Lampoon "Castle"

winter exams at Harvard. "New courses are selected, and even the full-year courses, heading into their second half, sometimes put on, like a new hat, a fresh professor. The days quietly lengthen; there is a snowstorm or two. . . . The elms are seen to be shaped like fountains. . . . the brick buildings, the arched gates, the archaic lecterns, and the barny mansions along Brattle Street dawn upon the freshman as a heritage he temporarily possesses. . . . The letters from home dwindle in importance. The hours open up. There is more time."

As you continue along Mt. Auburn Street, glance up Holyoke Street, where, in 1638, the first printing shop in America opened for business **(15)**.

WILLIAM FAULKNER (1897–1962) is not a writer ordinarily associated with Cambridge. Nevertheless, an obscure Faulkner-inspired memorial is on Anderson Bridge **(16)**, a ten-minute walk down John F. Kennedy Street toward the Charles River. In a little alcove on the east side of the bridge (next to the first street light) is a tiny plaque honoring the memory of the eldest son of a doomed Mississippi family.

In *Absalom, Absalom!* and *The Sound and the Fury*, Faulkner relentlessly tracks the disintegration of the Compsons, a fictional southern family of the old school. Quentin Compson, the only hope of the family, is sent to Harvard by his father because, as Quentin recollects in his last moments, "for you to go to harvard has been your mothers dream since you were born and no compson has ever disappointed a lady."

Alone and demoralized, Quentin commits suicide on June 2, 1910, by jumping into the Charles River. On the fifty-fifth "anniversary" of his death, three students placed a plaque in his honor beside the river to pay homage to Quentin's struggle with his lost ideals in a city far from home. The names of the students who responded to Faulkner's vivid portrait surfaced many years later, but they prefer anonymity. "Mystery is more appealing than facts," one of them explained.

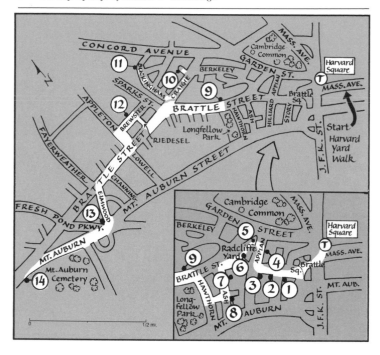

Brattle Street and Beyond

1. 42 Brattle Street (Margaret Fuller)
2. Brattle and Story streets (Longfellow: smithy forge)
3. 56 Brattle Street (Longfellow: smithy house)
4. 10 ½ Appian Way (John Berryman)
5. Radcliffe Yard (Gertrude Stein, Adrienne Rich)
6. Schlesinger Library
7. Off Brattle Street (Helen Keller and Anne Sullivan)
8. 14 Ash Street (T. S. Eliot)
9. 105 Brattle Street (H. W. Longfellow house)
10. 8 Craigie Circle (Vladimir Nabokov)
11. 29 Buckingham Street (T. W. Higginson)
12. 35 Brewster Street (Robert Frost)
13. 33 Elmwood Avenue (James Russell Lowell)
14. Mt. Auburn Cemetery (Harriet Jacobs, Lydia Maria Child)

Brattle Street and Beyond

"T" Stop: Harvard Square (Red Line)—ten minutes from Park Street.
   Brattle Square is around the corner from Harvard Square.
Restaurants: Sreets around Harvard and Brattle squares

THE BRATTLE STREET walk explores historic Brattle Street, takes a look at Radcliffe College, and goes on to Mount Auburn Cemetery. Here are the eighteenth-century clapboard houses of Cambridge, a smattering of poets' homes (Longfellow, Eliot, Lowell and others) and one of the most scenic cemeteries in the country.

Walking time is about three hours if you walk to the cemetery and back, or one hour if you go only as far as the Longfellow House and back. Public transportation to Mount Auburn Cemetery leaves from the Harvard Square "T" stop underground. Taxis are available in Harvard Square.

Brattle Street, which starts in Brattle Square, was known as Tory Row in the 1700s. Wealthy royalist families bought up huge tracts of land bordering on the street and built spacious, sturdy clapboard houses. The Tories had to pick up and leave on the eve of the Revolution, but many of their houses are still standing.

The clapboard house at 42 Brattle Street (1) was built in 1727 by William Brattle, a wealthy Tory officer. MARGARET FULLER, whom you met on the Downtown Boston walk, moved here with her parents in 1832. Her scholarly achievements so impressed Harvard professors that she was the first woman invited to use the college library.

The benign influence of nineteenth-century resident HENRY WADSWORTH LONGFELLOW (1807–1882) has long hovered over Brattle Street, drawing writers—and poets in particular—to settle, however briefly, nearby. You can visit Longfellow's home later on this walk.

Dexter Pratt, Longfellow's "village blacksmith," had his workshop on the northwest corner of Story Street, where a plaque marks the location of his forge (2). Though the city has encroached on this once tree-shaded spot, Longfellow's lines capture a segment of nineteenth-century daily life.

> Under a spreading chestnut-tree
> The village smithy stands;
> The smith, a mighty man is he,
> With large and sinewy hands,
> And the muscles of his brawny arms
> Are strong as iron bands.

The blacksmith's home at 56 Brattle Street (3) is now a bakery-cafe with an outdoor terrace. It is marked by one of the oval blue-and-white signs that identify Cambridge's historic buildings. Read them to get a picture of the architecture and occupants of early Cambridge.

The modern **LOEB DRAMA CENTER** is in the next block, across Hilliard Street. The Loeb, built in 1960, was Harvard's extremely tardy reply to drama professor George Pierce Baker's defection to Yale in 1925 (see the Around Harvard Yard walk).

On the other side of Brattle Street, Hilliard becomes Appian Way. Walk down to No. 10 ½, where the poet **JOHN BERRYMAN** (1914–1972) lived during the 1940-41 academic year, when he taught at Harvard (4). Years later he wrote a long poem inspired by the life of poet Anne Bradstreet, who lived in Harvard Square three hundred years earlier.

Eileen Simpson, who later married Berryman, once spent the weekend here. In her memoir, *Poets in Their Youth*, she describes the tiny addition to 10 Appian Way as an "oversized playhouse" that was "outrageously uncomfortable." Tucked beside a white clapboard house, the structure is just barely visible behind a high fence.

Simpson's book touches closely on the lives of Berryman,

Robert Lowell, and **DELMORE SCHWARTZ** (1913–1966), who lived at 20 Ellery Street beyond the Fogg Museum for several years. Saul Bellow used Delmore Schwartz as the real-life model for a fictional poet named Van Humboldt Fleisher in his novel *Humboldt's Gift*. A close friend of Schwartz, Bellow recreated incidents in Schwartz's life so graphically that a future biographer of the poet was able to rely on their accuracy.

As you look down Appian Way from Brattle Street, you will see the edge of the Cambridge Common, where George Washington took command of his army of volunteers in July 1775.

The next stop is the Radcliffe Yard **(5)**, a quiet oasis with a garden off to one side. Enter through the gate just down Appian Way.

RADCLIFFE COLLEGE was founded in 1879 "to give private tuition to properly qualified young women who desire to pursue advanced studies in Cambridge." The instruction, provided by Harvard professors, was to be of "no . . . lower grade than that given in Harvard College." Soon nicknamed the Harvard Annex, the college was formally named in 1894 in honor of Ann Radcliffe (later Lady Mowlson) who, in 1643, was the first woman to donate a scholarship to Harvard. Although Radcliffe has never had its own faculty, and students have always received a Harvard education, instruction did not become fully coeducational until after the Second World War.

The college is an independent institution, supporting a variety of programs. Of particular interest in the Radcliffe Yard is the **SCHLESINGER LIBRARY (6)**, a world-renowned repository of manuscripts, books, photographs and other documents relating to the history of women in America. The Schlesinger's culinary collection is one of the country's finest.

GERTRUDE STEIN (1874–1946) spoke at Agassiz Theatre in the Radcliffe Yard long after she studied at the college in the late 1890s. Stein wrote novels, plays and opera librettos in an unpunctuated, provocative style ("Rose is a rose is a rose is a rose.") that shocked some and delighted others.

While she was at Radcliffe, Gertrude Stein studied with philosopher William James. She emigrated to France, where she lived with her secretary and friend Alice B. Toklas. Toklas gained a certain notoriety when Stein wrote her own autobiography and then called it *The Autobiography of Alice B. Toklas*. A true avant-garde writer, Stein loved to experiment. After all, she remarked, "If you can do something, why do it?"

ADRIENNE RICH (b. 1929) published a prize-winning book of poems as a Radcliffe undergraduate. Author of several books of poetry, Rich has become a forceful advocate for feminism. In *Of Woman Born*, Rich explores, this time in prose, the institution of "motherhood in a patriarchal culture," comparing her own upbringing in a father-dominated household with that of Louisa May Alcott, whom you met on Beacon Hill.

The residence of Radcliffe's president, 76 Brattle Street, is across the street as you exit by the gate to the left of Schlesinger Library. To the right of the president's brick home is a small parking area that almost hides a path leading to a fountain placed against the rear wall of a graduate-student residence **(7)**. Visits to the quiet quadrangle are permitted, despite the "private" sign.

The fountain, which includes a plaque in braille, was dedicated by Radcliffe graduate **HELEN KELLER** (1880–1968) in honor of her teacher and companion Anne Sullivan. Keller, who lost both her sight and her hearing before she was two years old, seemed doomed to a silent and solitary existence until the skills and devotion of Anne Sullivan catapulted her into a life of achievement.

In her application to Radcliffe in 1900, Keller wrote, "I realize that the obstacles in the way of my receiving a college education are very great—to others they may even seem insurmountable; but dear Sir, a true soldier does not acknowledge defeat before the battle." In 1955, she was the first woman to receive an honorary degree from Harvard.

The fountain commemorates the day the young Helen connected the word *water*—"spelled" into one hand by her teacher—

with the liquid in which she had immersed her other hand. In *The Story of My Life*, Keller writes that at this moment "the mystery of language was revealed to me. I knew then that 'w-a-t-e-r' meant the wonderful cool something that was flowing over my hand. That living word awakened my soul, gave it light, hope, joy, set it free!"

T. S. ELIOT (1888–1965) lived at 14 Ash Street **(8)** in 1913-14, while he was teaching at Harvard. Eliot, who was born in St. Louis, was not in Cambridge long. Although he came from a family with strong New England roots, by 1927 he was a citizen of Great Britain, where he reigned as one of the most erudite and honored poets of his generation.

In 1917 Eliot published his first book of poetry, which includes the quotable "Love Song of J. Alfred Prufrock." Other poems in this book poke not-so-gentle fun at the prim and peculiar habits of New England women he calls "Cousin Harriet," "Aunt Helen," and "Cousin Nancy." In "The *Boston Evening Transcript*," Eliot mocks the slavish dependence of his older Beacon Hill relatives and friends on the editorial opinions of this decorous newspaper, well known for never printing a breath of scandal.

The **LONGFELLOW HOUSE** at 105 Brattle **(9)**, is well worth a visit. Don't neglect **LONGFELLOW PARK** across the street where, at the very end, you will find a statue of Longfellow backed by several of his heroes and heroines carved in bas-relief—a puzzle in identification for fans. On the way back you will be rewarded by a superb view of the house, which served as Washington's headquarters in the early months of the Revolutionary War.

When Longfellow came to Harvard in 1837 as professor of modern languages, he rented a room in this house from Mrs. Elizabeth Craigie, whose husband had recently died bankrupt. Six years later, when Longfellow married Bostonian Fanny Appleton, his father-in-law made them a present of the house. In July 1861, following a custom of the times, Fanny snipped some curls from her daughters' hair to keep as mementos in packets closed with sealing wax. As she struck a match to melt the wax, her filmy summer dress caught fire. Fanny rushed into her husband's study where Longfellow threw a rug around her to extinguish the flames. Longfellow's face was badly burned in his futile attempt to rescue her. Fanny, who never spoke again, was buried on the anniversary of their wedding day. Eighteen years later (exactly the length of time the couple had been married) Longfellow wrote mournfully of the "cross of snow" he had carried "upon my breast . . . since the day she died."

The poignant stories and hypnotic rhythms of Longfellow's long narrative poems were wildly successful. "The Courtship of Miles Standish," describing the romance between Priscilla Mullins and John Alden ("Why don't you speak for yourself, John?"), sold ten thousand copies in London and another five thousand in America on the day it appeared. "The Song of Hiawatha" ("By the shores of Gitche Gumee, / By the shining Big-Sea Water") served for a time as a primer for beginning readers, and "Paul Revere's Ride" is an American classic.

Longfellow's popularity during his heyday rivaled that of

Home of Henry Wadsworth Longfellow

modern media stars. One summer more than fifty thousand people went to Cambridge just to gaze at his house. While his poetry is not revered today as it once was, Longfellow is a major figure in America's literary history—a poet whose inner voice was in tune with the age and whose lyric grace still commands respect.

While you are resting in Longfellow Park, read about two prominent literary figures who lived in the area. The map shows an optional walk to their homes, marked (10) and (11).

VLADIMIR NABOKOV (1899–1977) emigrated to the United States in 1940. Three years later he settled in an apartment house at 8 Craigie Circle (10). He would have liked a job with Harvard, but accepted a post at Wellesley College, where he electrified his students with brilliant lectures on Russian and European literature. He did manage one Harvard position, however, as a part-time research fellow in entomology at the Museum of Comparative Zoology, where, he noted, "I am custodian of these absolutely fabulous collections."

Since that time, literary critics have carefully tracked the references to butterflies that permeate his work. Nabokov himself notes in one edition of his novel, *Lolita:* "Every summer my wife and I go butterfly hunting. The specimens are deposited at scientific institutions such as the Museum of Comparative Zoology at Harvard. . . . The locality labels pinned under these butterflies will be a boon to some twenty-first-century scholar with a taste for recondite biography. It was at such of our headquarters as Telluride, Colorado . . . that *Lolita* was energetically resumed in the evenings or on cloudy days."

THOMAS WENTWORTH HIGGINSON (1823–1911) lived at 29 Buckingham Street (11). Higginson, a biographer and advocate for women's rights entered quite by chance into an unusual correspondence with EMILY DICKINSON (1830–1886), who lived in Amherst, Massachusetts. In 1862 Higginson wrote an essay in the *Atlantic Monthly* giving advice to any hypothetical "young contributor" who might wish to submit material to the magazine. Soon after, he received poems and a letter from an unknown young woman who asked, "Are you too deeply occupied to say if my verse is alive?"

Higginson was intrigued, but suggested to Emily Dickinson that she delay publication. Her poems, he wrote a friend, reminded him of "skeleton leaves, so pretty, but too delicate—not strong enough to publish." In fact, he did not know how to react to this strange creature who sent him oddly phrased letters about herself. "Sir," she wrote, " . . . I sing, as the boy does by the burying ground—because I am afraid. . . . I have a brother and Sister—My mother does not care for thought—and Father, too busy with his briefs, to notice what we do—He buys me many books but begs me not to read them—because he fears they joggle the mind."

Dickinson and Higginson continued to correspond, and he is often criticized for not recognizing her genius. In his defense, it is not hard to imagine that a critic accustomed to Longfellow's flowing verse would find Dickinson's poetry "curiously indifferent to all conventional rules."

> To make a prairie it takes a clover and one bee,
> And revery.
> The revery alone will do
> If bees are few.

Higginson, who never quite believed that the public would accept Dickinson's poems as she wrote them, changed words and altered rhymes when he published the first edition of her work a few years after her death. Emily Dickinson, like Walt Whitman, was finally recognized as a great American poet who deliberately rejected the old forms in favor of a personal vision.

At this point, intrepid walkers may carry on along tree-shaded streets to the homes of Robert Frost and James Russell Lowell, and to Mount Auburn Cemetery. The cemetery is a half-hour's walk from Longfellow Park, and you can return by a trolley-bus after strolling around the grounds.

ROBERT FROST (1874–1963), yet another of the poets along

this path, lived off and on at 35 Brewster Street **(12)**. "Last
November," wrote Robert Lowell the year Frost died, "I walked by
his house on Brewster Street. . . . Its narrow gray wood was a town
cousin of the farmhouses he wrote about, and stood on some middle
ground between luxury and poverty. It was a traveler from the last
century that had inconspicuously drifted over the customs border of
time."

Frost left America in 1912 to settle in England, where his
first two books were published just before his fortieth birthday. He
returned to America in 1915, in time to receive the recognition he
deserved. Although he is known for the poems he wrenched out of
his years of farm life in New Hampshire and Vermont, Frost is more
than the quintessential New Englander. Using local settings and
traditional poetic forms, he explores universal themes: man's rela-
tion to the natural world and the joys and sorrows of human
experience.

JAMES RUSSELL LOWELL (1819–1891) was born at 33
Elmwood Avenue **(13)** and lived there most of his life. On sunny
summer afternoons Lowell liked to play the farmer and pitch hay in
his back meadow. Elmwood, his impressive yellow clapboard house,
is now the residence of the president of Harvard University.

Although Lowell was an admired poet in his day, he is better
remembered now as a witty and incisive Harvard professor of literature, host to all the prominent writers who set foot in Boston and
Cambridge, and as the first editor of the *Atlantic Monthly*.

Lowell, "an undersized gentleman in a Highland cloak," used
to leave this spacious house in the morning and walk along the river
and over the bridge to his office on Tremont Street in Boston. One
windy day, his hat blew off into the Charles River. Not too serious an
event perhaps, except that Lowell had the habit of stuffing
manuscripts under his hat, rather than carrying them. Page after page
of handwritten submissions followed the hat into the river.
Fortunately for the magazine, if not for the writers, Lowell had read
the manuscripts the night before and had already rejected all of them.

AMY LOWELL (1874–1925), who lived in neighboring Brookline, was another member of this talented family. She allied herself with the group of imagist poets led by Ezra Pound. Their manifesto declared that "new rhythms," exact "images" and "concentration" were the "very essence of poetry."

Amy Lowell was an independent, strong-willed, cigar-smoking woman who rather enjoyed the controversy her unusual behavior aroused. She turned the clock around, sleeping during the day on a mattress made from two dozen pillows. Rising at three in the afternoon, she entertained at an eight o'clock dinner and then wrote from midnight to early morning. Her brother Lawrence, a president of Harvard, dealt with the situation in his own way. "I'll say anything I want about my sister," he remarked, "but by Jove I won't allow anyone else to."

After viewing Elmwood, cross the street at the dead-end sign and wend your way across three pedestrian crosswalks to the far side. Turn right and walk up to **MOUNT AUBURN CEMETERY (14)**, which has been a favorite excursion place since its consecration in 1831. When Charles Dickens was in town, his Boston friends couldn't wait to take him there on a Sunday carriage ride. This beautiful spot was the first cemetery in America to be planned as a garden and is now known worldwide for its collection of unusual shrubs and trees. Birdwatchers flock here in the early mornings, particularly in late spring when crabapple, dogwood and rhododendron bloom on the hillsides.

Ask at the office for a map of the cemetery. Fourteen of the "noted persons" on the official list are mentioned in this guide. One woman buried here whose name is not on the list is **HARRIET A. JACOBS** (1813–1897), the author of a fiercely proud autobiography, *Incidents in the Life of a Slave Girl*. Her grave is located not far from the front entrance on Clethra Path in Section B8 of the map.

Born a North Carolina slave in 1813, Harriet Jacobs refused as a teenager to yield to the sexual advances of her owner. She later entered into a relationship with a man by whom she had two children, one of whom is buried beside her. Repeated threats from her owner ended in her supposed escape to the North. Actually, she hid for almost seven years curled up under the eaves of her grandmother's house.

Jacobs, who had learned to read and write as a child, never lost control of her life. She first planned her children's escape, then created a false trail by writing letters that others mailed from addresses in northern cities. Finally, she, too, managed to escape. Until her freedom was purchased in 1852, she lived in constant fear of recapture. She worked as a dressmaker in Boston's North End and later ran a boarding house in Cambridge.

Her remarkable story, which was first printed in Boston, was edited by **LYDIA MARIA CHILD** (1802–1880), a prominent Massachusetts writer whose own antislavery publications had caused her to be ostracized from many homes and literary circles. Even the enlightened Boston Athenaeum library, which supported other abolitionists, rescinded Mrs. Child's borrowing privileges after her essay "Appeal in Favor of that Class of Americans Called Africans" was published. No amount of scorn could, however, keep Lydia Maria Child from fighting against the "wild beast of slavery."

The Charles River in Cambridge

Further Reading

The books listed below touch on different aspects of literature and history in Boston and Cambridge. Other books are mentioned in the text. Libraries and bookstores can provide excellent biographies of major literary figures.

Amory, Cleveland. *The Proper Bostonians*. New York: E. P. Dutton, 1947.

Bahne, Charles. *The Complete Guide to Boston's Freedom Trail*. Cambridge: Newtowne Publishing, 1985.

Bentinck-Smith, William, ed. *The Harvard Book*. Cambridge: Harvard University Press, 1957.

Brooks, Van Wyck. *The Flowering of New England*. New York: E. P. Dutton, 1936.

_____. *New England: Indian Summer, 1865-1915*. New York: E. P. Dutton, 1940.

Cather, Willa. *Not Under Forty*. New York: Alfred A. Knopf, 1922. Reprint. Lincoln, NE: University of Nebraska Press, 1988.

Ehrlich, Eugene, and Gorton Carruth, eds. *The Oxford Illustrated Literary Guide to the United States*. New York: Oxford University Press, 1982.

Forbes, Esther. *Paul Revere & the World He Lived In*. Boston: Houghton Mifflin Co., 1942.

Harris, John. *Historic Walks in Cambridge*. Chester, CT: The Globe Pequot Press, 1986.

_____. *Historic Walks in Old Boston*. Chester, CT: The Globe Pequot Press, 1982.

Jones, Howard Mumford and Bessie Z. Jones, eds. *The Many Voices of Boston, 1630–1975*. Boston: Little, Brown and Co., 1975.

McCord, David. *About Boston*. Boston: Little, Brown and Co., 1948.

Matthiessen, F. O. *American Renaissance*. New York: Oxford University Press, 1941.

Miller, Perry. *The New England Mind: from Colony to Province*. Cambridge: Harvard University Press, 1953.

Morison, Samuel Eliot. *One Boy's Boston, 1887–1901*. Boston: Houghton Mifflin Co., 1962. Reprint. Boston: Northeastern University Press, 1983.

Seaburg, Carl. *Boston Observed*. Boston: Beacon Press, 1971.

Tharp, Louise Hall. *The Peabody Sisters of Salem*. Boston: Little, Brown and Co., 1950.

WPA Guide to Massachusetts. Reprint of *The WPA Guide to Massachusetts* (1937), with a new introduction by Jane Holtz Kay. New York: Pantheon Books, 1983.

Index